Muhammad Ali, The Confederate Flag, and Other Essays

Dwayne Wong (Omowale)

Wong (Omowale)

CONTENTS

1

AFRICA: LAND OF SAVAGERY & VIOLENCE

"And this is the role that the press plays, if you study back in history different wars, always the press, whenever a country that's in power wants to step unjustly and invade someone else's property, they use the press to make it appear that the area that they are about to invade is filled with savages, or filled with people who have gone berserk, or they are raping white women, molesting nuns, they use the same old tactic year in and year out."
-Malcolm X

One of the justifications for the slave trade and colonization was the idea that African people are savage and violent, and that it was the job of the Europeans to civilize these savages. The numerous examples of war and violence in post-colonial Africa is often taken to be proof that African people were the same savages that European propaganda depicted and that without the guiding influence of Western colonialism African nations merely reverted to their previous state of savagery; that Africans experienced a state of atavism. Indeed, the picture of Africa in the years following independence is a grim one.

Following independence from European colonial rule Africa has been wrecked by a number of violent conflicts. Among these include the civil war in Sierra Leone, in which the Revolutionary United Front inflicted a number of brutalities on the civilian population. This included amputating limbs and sexual assaults. One of the most gruesome aspects of this war was that the RUF forced children to serve as soldiers. This war ravaged Sierra Leone for over ten years. Between 1989 and 2003, Liberia fought two civil wars in which hundreds of thousands of people were killed. Much like the civil war in Sierra Leone, in the Liberian wars children were forced to serve as soldiers, and committed a number of atrocities.

Côte d'Ivoire also endured two civil wars, the first of which lasted from 2002 to 2007. A second civil war broke out in 2010. The Congo was the location of two major wars from 1996 to 2003. The Second Congo War was particularly devastating. Nigeria fought a civil war in 1967 that resulted in the death of a million people. The Sudan suffered a civil war that lasted from 1955 to 1972, followed by a second civil war that lasted from 1983 to 2005. These are only some of the many conflicts that Africa has been engulfed in since gaining independence from the European colonial powers.

These conflicts helped to confirm the image that the colonists depicted of Africa. They depicted Africans as savages that were incapable of governing themselves. The reality of the situation is much more complex than this, however. The Africa that Europeans encountered was not a land wrecked with civil wars, poverty, and starvation. Those things were the legacies of European colonial rule. The Africa that Europeans encountered was far from a land filled with savagery and violence.

European accounts of their interactions with Africans attest to the hospitality that the Europeans were greeted with. W.E.B. Du Bois writes of the hospitality in Africa:

> In disposition the Negro is among the most lovable of men. Practically all the great travelers, who have spent any considerable time in Africa testify to this, and pay deep tribute to the kindness with which they were received. One has but to remember the classic story of Mungo Park, the strong expressions of Livingstone, the words of Stanley, and hundreds of others to realize this.

One European in Africa observed the customs of hospitality In Africa and recorded:

> The law of hospitality is obstructive of industry. If there is provision in the country, a man who wants it has only to find out who has got any, and he must have his share. If he enters any man's house during his repast, and gives him the usual salutation, the man must invite him to partake. Thus, whatever

2

abundance a man may get by assiduity, will be shared by the lazy; and thus they seldom calculate for more than necessaries.

This is interesting because this particular European sees the practice of African hospitality as "obstructive" and that this was sharing with the lazy. That such hospitality fostered laziness was not the case for the generosity of the society went both ways. There is a proverb in Swahili which states: "Treat your guest as a guest for two days; on the third day give him a hoe!" Very often the guest would not wait until the third day to take the hoe because he understood that it was expected of him to give something in return to his host. The hospitality of this social system went both ways. In *The Groundings with My Brothers*, Walter Rodney explains:

> Numerous reports attest to the hospitality of African communities. Within any village or chiefdom, the codes of hospitality and a spirit of charity prevented the extremes of poverty and abandonment which one finds in richer and supposedly more mature societies. The African extended-family was in itself an agency for mutual aid and welfare; and the family connections led to the clan, where a similar pattern unfolds [...] The greater the status of the individual, the greater his obligation to have an open house for all, although he did get something in return, for the reciprocal exchange of gifts was a common practice.

This hospitality in Africa was a common feature in the society's structure that had existed even before the Europeans arrived. For example, the warlike Bijagos, who conducted raids on their neighbors, welcomed all who came to their islands as friends and guests. Wilfrid D. Hambly recorded that among the Ovimbundu when a woman marries into a family she is told by her parents, "We should like to hear that you are hospitable; give food to your husbands' relatives when they visit you." African hospitality was even extended to animals, as the Beafada prohibited the killing of birds that were perched on trees nearby Beafada homes because these birds were viewed as guests to whom they could do no harm.

W.E.B. Du Bois also experienced this hospitality firsthand for himself. He wrote that Africans "bring in intimate human knowledge that the West misses, sinking the individual in the social. Africans know fewer folk, but know them infinitely better. Their intertwined communal souls, therefore, brook no poverty nor prostitution—these things are to them un-understandable." Upon arriving at a village, Du Bois describes: "Neither London, nor Paris, nor New York has anything of its delicate, precious beauty. It was a town of the Veys and done in cream and pale purple—still, clean, restrained, tiny, complete. It was no selfish place, but the central abode of fire and hospitality, clean-swept for wayfarers, and best seats were bare. They quite expected visitors, morning, noon, and night; and they gave our hands a quick, soft grasp and talked easily. Their manners were better than those of Park Lane or Park Avenue. Oh, much better and more natural."

The Africa that Du Bois encountered was one of hospitality and humanity, and both aspects existed on a level in Africa that was not equaled in the much more "sophisticated" United States. Du Bois also spoke of how well-manned the children were. Du Bois wrote: "Come to Africa, and see well-bred and courteous children, playing happily and never sniffling and whining." Du Bois discovered an Africa that was far from something to be scorned at or to be dismissed. He found an Africa that he felt the European world could have learned much from, but Du Bois was also aware of the fact that Europeans found the idea of learning anything from Africa to be a laughable one and that they would rather defend their own social problems by arguing that: "Poverty cannot be abolished. Democracy and firm government are incompatible. Prostitution is world old and inevitable."

Aside from the hospitality, European accounts of Africa also describe a land where there was a great sense of security. The Greeks were very impressed by the humanity of African society. Stobaeus wrote that the Ethiopians do not have doors on their houses and that they do not steal anything that is left out on the streets. Mungo Park said that the Djolas were barbaric, but even he had to admit that he was able to leave his items unattended and the Djolas stole nothing. Even with all the horror stories about Shaka, the Europeans who visited Zululand during his reign were struck by the security and lack of theft that they found. Upon witnessing the march of some of Shaka's regiments, Henry Francis Fynn had to write of the Zulus: "It was a most exciting scene, surprising to us, who could not have imagined that a nation termed 'savages' could be so disciplined and kept in order." This lack of theft in Africa was something that even Arab travelers in the Western Sudan commented on.

Rev. Samuel Johnson stated of the Yoruba people of the Oyo Kingdom:

> As regards the social virtues, the ancient Oyos or Yorubas proper were very virtuous, loving and kind. Theft was rare as also fornication in spite of the scantiness or often times complete absence of clothing to which they were accustomed. Friendship was more sincere.

Most ironic is that when the Europeans first arrived in Africa they found a society that was hospitable, friendly, and secure. Although they would later paint Africans as bloodthirsty cannibalistic savages, the fact that Africans were so welcoming in the first place is what allowed for the European exploitation of African people. Walter Rodney comments on this irony when he points out:

> Africans approached their earliest European acquaintances in the same hospitable and charitable manner that was normal in dealings among themselves. They called the white men 'honoured guests', they gave them protection and love, they plied them with gifts; it took Africans some time to realise that Europeans worshipped strange gods called Money and Profit.

There was crime in Africa, and we find that the way in which Africans dealt with crime was generally more tolerant and more humane than what was done in Europe. Traditional African societies typically did not have jails; they did not even have a word that meant jail in their languages. This was because the wrongdoer was not locked up as punishment.

We must also keep in mind that capital punishment in African society was much less frequent than it was in Europe. In feudal England alone there were 300 offenses for which one could be killed, but in many African societies there were only a handful of crimes which were punishable by death. Walter Rodney described punishment in West Africa as follows:

> In the opening years of the sixteenth century, murder alone was punishable by death among the Bulloms, while the Temnes had no capital offences. Indeed, on the whole West African coast, capital punishment was a rarity, in distinct contrast to Europe. The principal penalties were in the form of fines. Adultery, for instance, was easily resolved by the offending male paying agreed damages. Deprivation of liberty seems to have been entirely unknown, but with the advent of the Atlantic slave trade Africans were led to become parties in plots which resulted in the lifelong deprivation of the liberty of their fellows.

The traditional justice system of the Acholi/Luo in Uganda gives us a detailed example of a traditional African judicial system. In Uganda, the Lord's Resistance Army (LRA) led by Joseph Kony, was known for committing all sorts of atrocities. Their campaign to overthrow the government and replace it with a regime based on the Ten Commandments became a campaign that involved massacring and mutilating the civilian population. They also abducted children and used them as soldiers.

It was decided that for the war to end all those who committed the atrocities had to be forgiven. LRA rebels were given full amnesty. The community used traditional cleansing and forgiveness rituals. This traditional judicial system is known as Mato Oput (reconciliation). Of Mato Oput, Rev. Mcleod Baker Ochola states:

If capital punishment were deemed appropriate for such offender, he/she is kept in isolation and confinement, as a wrong and dangerous element to the community or society. If it is life imprisonment, the offender would be put out of circulation from the larger society for ever. This is meant to serve justice for the victims and/or survivors of the offence. Presumably, it is also supposed to serve justice for the society at large as some form of deterrence. But have these forms of punishment succeeded to expand justice and reduce crimes?

The story behind the creation of Mato Oput is an interesting one. According to oral tradition the practice of Mato Oput traces back to the separation of two brothers named Labongo and Gipir. In Luo society the spear is not only a weapon, but also a symbol of power, authority, and leadership. Labongo, being the elder son, was given the ancestral spear by his elderly father. During the ceremony, Labongo was made to swear on his ancestors that he would guard the ancestral spear with his life.

One morning an elephant wandered into a garden of cowpeas that belonged to Labongo. Labongo was away hunting at the time, but Gipir was made aware of the elephant and rushed to protect the garden. In a hurry, Labongo grabbed the ancestral spear and threw the spear at the elephant, wounding the creature. The elephant ran away with the spear still stuck in it. It was only after the elephant escaped that Gipir realized what he had done. Labongo returned home to find out that the elephant had escaped with the ancestral spear. Labongo was enraged by this and demanded that Gipir retrieve the spear. Gipir pleaded with his brother to accept a replacement spear, but Labongo refused to accept anything but the same spear that he had sworn to guard with his life.

Labongo ordered his brother to find the spear and not to come back home without it. Gipir was gone for months, which led some to believe that Gipir may have been killed in the forest. Gipir had in fact found the dead elephant and retrieved the spear, but he was weary and sick from his journey. Gipir came upon an old woman in the forest who nursed him back to health. She gave Gipir food, new sandals, and some royal beads.

Gipir finally returned home. Women and children greeted him, but Gipir walked by them without even acknowledging them. He went straight to his brother to deliver the spear. Before Labongo could respond, Gipir stormed off in anger. Months went by after this incident and one day some of his family came to admire the royal beads that Gipir came back with. As he was threading the beads some of them fell to the ground and one of Labongo's daughters swallowed it.

Gipir brought the child to Labongo, demanding to have his beads back immediately. Labongo begged his brother to accept a replacement bead, but Gipir refused. Gipir also refused to wait until the girl had passed the beads out. Labongo immediately became ashamed when he remembered how he had ignored his brother's pleas months earlier. Labongo ordered that his daughter be cut open so that the beads could be removed. She died as a result of this. This incident eventually caused the separation of the two brothers.

It is this tragic tale that helped to shape the Luo understanding of justice and forgiveness. It was the inability of the two brothers to forgive each other that led to the tragic, but avoidable death of Labongo's daughter, so Mato Oput developed from the understanding that forgiveness and reconciliation are key elements to dealing with disputes and conflicts.

The first step in Mato Oput is truth telling, which is "rigorous, straightforward and transparent." Rev. MacBaker Ochola describes: "Through public confession, the offender community becomes vulnerable and guilty for the crimes committed by one of its members. This is the fundamental basis for community-based collective responsibility of the offender community."

The second step is that reparations are paid to the victims and survivors. The compensation is paid to demonstrate the sincerity of the offender. The next step is that the offender community and the offended community share food together. MacBaker Ochola explains that in the Luo community "sharing of food with one another is a fundamental fellowship." The fourth and final step is the drinking of bitter herbs, which is done to symbolize drinking up all the bitterness of the conflict. The bitter juice, which is obtained from an oput tree, is poured into a calabash and drank by selected participants.

For the final step in the process of Mato Oput, three or four representatives are selected to represent the community. In the selection process, an aunt must always be selected as one of the representatives. MacBaker Ochola gives the explanation that in Luo culture the aunt holds a special position in the family and that she has the final say in all matters relating to the family.

Revenge is justifiable in Luo culture, but only if the offender refuses to accept responsibility for their crime. The offender's refusal to accept responsibility is taken as a challenge to the community and in this situation the community has "lapir" or "just cause." The concept of revenge for unpunished crimes is so ingrained in Luo culture that there is a belief that if a person is killed by an unknown assailant, the victim will return as a vengeful spirit to get revenge against the murderer and the community in which the murderer lives.

Certain crimes were outside the realm of Mato Oput. For example, gang rape was not known among the Acholi, therefore Mato Oput did not cover such a crime. Other crimes that were not covered by Mato Oput were father-daughter incest and cannibalism. These crimes were so grave that they were attributed to the Ogre (Obibi), as such crimes went beyond normal humanity to the realm of the demons. Overall, the Acholi society was one where there was little theft or violence. Ochola explains:

> Because of the Luo cultural and traditional prohibition of theft, the traditional Luo house had a very simple door called 'kikka' which was not burglar proof because there were no burglars in traditional Luo society. Kikka was not meant to keep out violence because traditional Luo society was non-violent. A child had no problem to enter a house since the kikka could easily be pulled either way, right or left. Kikka,

therefore, was the symbol of a non-violent and peaceful community.

We also find that African societies provided for some of its most vulnerable members. The kingdom of Monomotapa, for example, had a very well-organized social welfare system that took care of the disabled. A Portuguese traveler named Antonio Bocarro stated that the king of Monomotapa "shows great charity to the blind and maimed, for these are called the king's poor, and have land and revenues for their subsistence, and when they wish to pass through the kingdoms, wherever they come food and drink are given to them at the public cost as long as they remain there, and when they leave that place to go to another they are provided with what is necessary for their journey, and a guide, and some one to carry their wallet to the next village. In every place where they come there is the same obligation, under penalty that those who fail therein shall be punished by the king."

This is not to give one the wrong impression that Africa was a type of utopian paradise before Europeans arrived. Africans fought bloody wars also. The Mali Empire expanded itself through conquering its neighbors. Likewise, Sonni Ali also expanded the Songhai Empire through a series of bloody conflicts, which included a siege on Djenné that lasted a few years and killed many people. The Egyptians inflicted many brutalities on their Nubian neighbors. Thutmose I of the 18th dynasty led a campaign into Kush in which he personally killed the king and then hung the king's body on his ship. But the majority of these conflicts were relatively short and the scale of destruction and damage was not what one saw in Europe. Furthermore, these conflicts never created problems for nations outside of Africa in the manner that Europe's imperial wars created conflicts outside of Europe.

We also find that in many cases these African wars were more or less short skirmishes that resulted in few if any deaths. In his book, *Destruction of Black Civilization*, Chancellor Williams gives us an interesting look at the nature of warfare in Africa. Williams writes:

The highly humane aspect of African warfare that puzzled

many Western visitors doubtlessly developed from the widespread recognition of lineage or kinship ties. For in the much heralded "tribal wars" the main objective was to overcome or frighten away the adversary, not to kill at all if it could be avoided. Hence the hideous masks and blood-curdling screams as they charged. Even when the enemy was defeated or completely surrounded, escape routes were provided, the victors pretending not to be aware of them. Indeed, there are reports of "rest periods," called when neither side seemed to be winning. At such times the warriors on both sides might meet at the nearest stream to refresh themselves, kid each other, and laugh at each others' jokes until the drums, gongs or trumpets sounded for the resumption of the battle.

Williams' statement cannot obscure the reality of the various violent and bloody wars that were fought in Africa, but his statement demonstrates that there were humane aspects in how Africans waged wars. Walter Rodney writes that wars in southern Africa "were hardly any more dangerous than a game of football in Latin America." He further notes that "a clan had traditional rivalry with another given clan. They knew each other well, and their champions fought in a spirit of festivity. One or two might have been killed, but then everyone went home until the rematch." European accounts of warfare in southern Africa during this time period also support what Rodney is saying. Theophilus Shepstone writes in his account of warfare in southern Africa:

The day was fixed beforehand, the men of the rival tribes met in battle on that day, and the result of the single encounter decided the quarrel. The few old men still living, who lived then, delight to tell how that in those good old times they did not fight to shed blood, or burn houses, or capture cattle, or destroy each other, but to settle a quarrel, and see which was the strongest [...] For then, unlike later times, they will touchingly add, "The sun that saw tribes fight never set till

11

their quarrel was ended."

Around the time when Shaka became ruler of the Zulus the warfare in southern Africa started to become much more intense and bloody. This period has generally been known as the Mfecane. This was a time of widespread warfare and chaos in southern Africa. The general perception is that this was caused by Shaka's violent expansion of the Zulu Empire, though the idea that Shaka and the Zulus were solely responsible for this has been challenged.

Shaka himself came to represent the tyranny and despotism of African kings, although the European accounts of Shaka tended to exaggerate the numbers of people that were killed in the wars against the Zulus. Nathaniel Isaacs wrote of Shaka:

> Chaka seems to have inherited no redeeming quality; in war he was an insatiable and exterminating savage, in peace an unrelenting and a ferocious despot, who kept his subjects in awe by his monstrous executions, and who was unrestrained in his bloody designs, because his people were ignorant, and knew not that they had power.

The Zulu king Cetshwayo was depicted in a similar light to his uncle Shaka. Chief among those that sought to paint a negative image of the Zulu king was a man named Sir B. Frere. Frere described Cetshwayo as a "cruel Sovereign" and an "irresponsible, bloodthirsty, and treacherous despot" who committed "atrocious barbarities." Frere even accuses Cetshwayo of trying to "emulate the sanguinary fame of his uncle Chaka." The *Guardian* challenged this depiction of Cetshwayo, reporting on the difficulties that the British faced in trying to capture Cetshwayo:

> Had Cetshwayo been a tyrant hated of the people and reigning over them against their will, it would never have taken all the labour we experienced to capture him.

Cornelius Vijn explained that in four years of living among the Zulu, he never heard the stories of Cetshwayo "killing many people" and he doubted that Cetshwayo had actually killed the number of people that he was said to have killed. He also expressed his disbelief at the thought that Cetshwayo was a "bloodthirsty tyrant." The picture that Vijn paints of Zululand is of a place that provided safety, security, and hospitality for him. He recorded that they were "friendly" towards him.

Vijn recorded two instances of killings which he noticed. The first of which was the death of a man who had committed adultery with one of the king's women. The man was pardoned on the first offence, but put to death when he committed another offense. The second instance was of a man named Umkogwana who was charged with witchcraft. Vijn added that he heard of cases where men were charged with witchcraft, but were not put to death. Vijn stated that Cetshwayo had to enforce the laws of his country and for this Vijn was grateful. Vijn stated that he owed his "safety to the order maintained by the King". Cetshwayo had ordered that anyone who dared to touch Vijn would be killed.

Another popular claim which is directly related to the notion of African savagery is the claim that Africans were cannibals. So not only are Africans violent and bloodthirsty, but they also devoured other humans. The whole idea of cannibalism is linked to notions of inferiority or lack of civilization, but we find that even in cases of cannibalism we cannot be so quick to dismiss a people as lacking civilization. Take for example the following account from Frobenius about some cannibalistic Africans that he encountered:

> These cannibal Bassonga were, according to the types we met with, one of those rare nations of the African interior which can be classed with the most esthetic and skilled, most discreet and intelligent of all those generally known to us as the so-called natural races. Before the Arabic and European invasion they did not dwell in 'hamlets,' but in towns with twenty or thirty thousand inhabitants, in towns whose highways were shaded by avenues of splendid palms planted at regular intervals and laid out with the symmetry of colonnades. Their

13

pottery would be fertile in suggestion to every art craftsman in Europe. Their weapons of iron were so perfectly fashioned that no industrial art from abroad could improve upon their workmanship. The iron blades were cunningly ornamented with damascened copper, and the hilts artistically inlaid with the same metal. Moreover, they were most industrious and capable husbandmen, whose careful tillage of the suburbs made them able competitors of any gardener in Europe. Their sexual and parental relations evidenced an amount of tact and delicacy of feelings unsurpassed among ourselves, either in the simplicity of the country or the refinements of the town. Originally their political and municipal system was organized on the lines of a representative republic. True, it is on record that these well-governed towns often waged an internecine warfare; but in spite of this it had been their invariable custom from time immemorial, even in times of strife, to keep the trade routes open and to allow their own and foreign merchants to go their ways unharmed. And the commerce of these nations ebbed and flowed along a road of unknown age, running from Itimbiri to Batubenge, about six hundred miles in length. This highway was destroyed by the "Missionaries of civilization" from Arabia only toward the close of the eighteenth century. But even in my own time there were still smiths who knew the names of places along that wonderful trade route driven through the heart of the "impenetrable forests of the Congo." For every scrap of imported iron was carried over it.

This leads us to the next point: what is the evidence of widespread cannibalism in Africa? The claim of cannibalism has been made more often than it has been proven. This has always been the problem concerning claims of cannibalism. Not only for Africans, but even the Native Americans were often accused of cannibalism. These claims were made by Europeans who had never witnessed cannibalism themselves, however. Christopher Columbus claimed that the Caribs were cannibals (the word cannibal is actually coined from the Caribs). Columbus had never witnessed these acts of cannibalism himself, but he helped to start a trend that would

14

continue for centuries. That trend is the Europeans accusing those that they conquered of being cannibals.

There's a report of the Mane invasion in the Upper Guinea Coast which stated that they ate some of their defeated enemies. According to the account of Andre Dornelas, the Manes were led by a woman named Macarico. She had offended the emperor in the city where she lived and was forced to leave. She took a large number of people with her, including friends and family. This group turned into an army. The army grew so big that they were forced to eat the people which they had defeated in order to sustain themselves. Some stories also state that the Manes would sometimes eat the flesh of their opponents to gain courage and ferocity. There was also a psychological aspect involved because such actions would frighten enemies, but it seems that this was done more as a fear tactic rather than being a part of their diets.

Emil Torday noted that the Basoko people of Central Africa ate the bodies of the dead because they believed that the soul remained in contact with the body after death and in doing so they acquired the virtues and strength of the dead. Torday explained that the Bankutu people ate the corpse of every slave so that the slaves could not haunt their master. This again was done as a ritual practice, rather than a dietary one.

Supposedly, the Fan people were cannibals that purchased slaves to eat them. Despite their reputation for cannibalism, Mary Kingsley was eager to meet the Fan people. She found that they were actually a friendly people. They taught her how to properly cook a snake—Kingsley stated that snake meat was one of the best meats one could find in Africa. Kingsley believed that the cannibalism of the Fan was no threat to white travelers, except for "the bother it gives one in preventing one's black companions from getting eaten."

While in a Fan town called Efoua, Kingsley was given a hut to sleep in. She was awakened by a terrible smell which was coming from some bags. She inspected the largest of the bags, pouring the contents of the bag into her hat. Inside the bag was "a human hand, three big toes, four eyes, two ears, and other portions of the human frame." Kingsley later learned that "although the Fans will eat their fellow friendly tribesfolk, yet they like to keep a little something belonging to them as a memento."

Kingsley noted that "Fan pottery, although rough and sunbaked, is artistic in form and ornamented," and that the Fan made outstanding nets. Of Fan iron, Kingsley stated that it deserved "especial notice for its excellence." Much like Frobenius' description of the cannibalistic Bassonga, Kingsley does not depict the Fan as a savage or inferior people, despite their reputation for cannibalism. Kingsley herself, like most European explorers in Africa, never witnessed this cannibalism firsthand, but was influenced by the reputation of cannibalism that she had heard prior to living among the Fan people.

As a boy Edward Alexander Powell read stories about African cannibals and "hankered to see a real live cannibal in the flesh." To his disappointment, he was told that "cannibalism is a thing of the past." His desire to find African cannibals was so great that he began to imagine that some of the Africans that he met were cannibals. This included Prempeh, the Asante king who was in exile at the time that Powell met him. Powell asserts that the British sent an expedition to Asante after Prempeh had selected a British commissioner for "one of his feasts," which was not the case at all. Powell concludes his impression of Prempeh by explaining that Prempeh "has killed and eaten more human beings, I suppose, than almost any man that ever lived." Powell offers zero evidence to support his claim.

Ota Benga, a Congolese man who was enslaved and brought to the United States where he was displayed at a zoo, was also alleged to have been a cannibal. One newspaper wrote: "His first wife excited the hunger of the rest of the tribe, and one day when Ota returned from hunting he learned that she had passed quietly away just before luncheon and that there was not so much as a sparerib for him." The reality is that Ota Benga's wife was killed by Europeans, but the perception that Africans were cannibals was so ingrained that accusations of cannibalism were often made in situations where there was zero evidence to support those charges.

Ironically, the Africans also believed that the Europeans were cannibals. Onboard the slave ships many Africans starved to death because they believed that the meat that was being served was actually the remains of other Africans who had previously been captured. Portuguese traders on the Guinea Coast were told by Africans that "the Christians ate human flesh and that all the slaves they bought they carried away to eat." Olaudah Equiano also shared this fear of being eaten. He records that after he was taken captive by whites, he asked the other captive Africans if the whites were planning to eat them. Even after they assured Equiano that the whites would not eat him, he was still very afraid of the whites. Mungo Park explained that the idea that whites cannibalized captive Africans terrified slaves in Africa.

To return to the issue of warfare in pre-colonial Africa, we find that warfare was not as savage and as bloody as is often portrayed. Even Shaka was much less of a despot and a monster than the popular images and stories of him suggest. The question this raises is that if the Europeans "civilized" the Africans, why then did African warfare become such bloody and destructive affairs? Take for example Nigeria's civil war. Walter Rodney called attention to the fact that at no point in Nigeria's pre-colonial history can one point to an example of the Ibos being massacred in large numbers by the Hausas. Rodney explains that there were wars, but these wars were not fought solely on the basis of ethnic differences. He describes the violence in post-colonial Nigeria as being the "product of administrative devices, of entrenched regional separations, of differential access by particular ethnic groups into the colonial economy and culture." Therefore the worst period of violence in Nigeria actually came after the Europeans supposedly civilized the Africans. Of course, Nigeria's very creation was steeped in violence and aggression in the first place.

The Rwanda Massacre is another example of how European presence led to an increase in violence. When the Europeans encountered the Hutu and Tutsi, the two groups were living together in relative peace. They were essentially one people practicing the same culture, but the Belgians found it convenient for their purposes to create division between the two groups. Rwanda was a German colony from 1894 until the end of World War I. Following Germany's defeat, Rwanda came under Belgium's control. The European colonialist saw the Tutsi as being superior to the Hutu and Twa. After sixty years of this ideology, many of the Tutsi began to believe that they were superior to the other ethnic groups in Rwanda.

To reinforce these divisions, the Belgians introduced ID cards in the 1930s. Rwanda retained these ID cards after gaining independence and it was not until after the genocide that this practice would be abolished. The ID cards were so successful in enforcing this division that Hutu leaders who wrote the 1957 "Hutu Manifest" spoke of the ID card categories as "races." This manifesto reflected the fact that by the 1950s the Hutu came to see themselves as a separate race from the Tutsi. In 1959, a pro-Hutu political party led an uprising that overthrew King Kigri V. This signaled the beginning of a period of violence that resulted in the deaths of thousands of Tutsis at the hands of the Hutu. Over 10,000 Tutsi were forced to flee to neighboring nations.

In 1962, Rwanda became independent under President Gregoire Kayibanda, who was one of the authors of the Hutu Manifesto. In the meanwhile, exiled Tutsi began launching attacks into Rwanda. These attacks were unsuccessful, but they did manage to increase the tensions between the two groups. After one failed invasion in 1963, the Rwandan government responded by massacring an estimated 10,000 Tutsi between December 1963 and 1964. These earlier conflicts would be the forerunner for the terrible genocide that would be committed 30 years later.

In 1973, Juvénal Habyarimana came to power in a coup. Like Kayibanda before him, Habyarimana retained the use of ID cards. In the early 1990s, European pressure forced the Rwandan government to allow political parties and freedom of press. This gave rise to radical pro-Hutu and pro-Tutsi sentiments. This was expressed in a particular "Hutu Power" newspaper that referred to Tutsi as an enemy. When Habyarimana called for a power-sharing government with the Tutsi he was denounced by Hutu Power supporters. This also increased the anti-Tutsi rhetoric of the Hutu Power leaders.

On April 6th, 1994, Habyarimana's plane was struck by a missile, killing the president and everyone else onboard. The identities of the killers were never revealed, although many believe that Habyarimana was killed by Hutu extremists that did not like his shift in policy concerning the Tutsi. Following the official announcement of Habyarimana's death, Hutu militiamen set up a roadblock and then checked the ID cards of anyone that passed by. Anyone who was found to be a Tutsi or a member of the opposition parties was killed. Making matters worse was when a popular radio station called for revenge against the Tutsi. Hutu extremists began massacring Tutsi and urged ordinary Hutu civilians to do the same.

In order to stop the slaughter, soldiers from the Rwandan Patriotic Front (RPF) political party began fighting the Hutu militias. After three months of fighting, the RPF finally defeated the Hutu militias and declared a cease-fire. During that period of time about 750,000 Tutsi and over 10,000 Hutu had been killed. Decades of tensions and violent conflicts between the Hutu and Tutsi had exploded into a large scale massacre. So successful were the Belgian divide and rule tactics that more than 30 years after gaining independence, Rwanda was not able to overcome these ethnic tensions. Perhaps most critical was the fact that the same ID cards that the Belgians introduced would play a central role in the genocide.

Another conflict in East Africa that has its roots in colonialism was the civil war in Djibouti. Djibouti was a French colony within French Somalia, before attaining independence in 1977. French colonial rule helped to create tensions between the Afar and Issa people. First of all, this was the first time that the Afar and Issa lived under the same political system. The two groups also had differing political ambitions. The Issa wanted immediate independence and some Issa wanted unification with Somalia. The Afar, on the other hand, generally wanted to remain under French rule, although there were some Afar that wanted independence, but rejected the idea of uniting with Somalia.

19

France was able to use these ethnic differences to prolong Djibouti's independence. It was clear that France did not wish for Djibouti to become independent given how France had threatened to withdraw assistance if the population of Djibouti voted in favor of independence during a 1966 referendum. The result of that referendum was that Djibouti remained a French colony and would remain so for more than a decade.

Upon achieving independence, the political differences between the Afar and Issa would create ethnic tensions in Djibouti that eventually resulted in a civil war in 1991 between the mostly Issa controlled government and Afar rebels. Much as was seen elsewhere in Africa, colonialism created a tense situation between different ethnic groups that helped lead to internal conflict. France had exploited the differences between the Issa and Afar in order to prolong colonial rule over Djibouti—Djibouti was in fact the last French colony in Africa to gain independence.

As was mentioned before, Africans did engage in warfare prior to the European presence, but colonialism changed the entire complexion of these conflicts. Through arbitrarily drawn borders and policies that divided different ethnic groups within the colonies, the European colonists helped to ensure an uneasy transition to independence. The same divide and conquer policies that helped the Europeans maintain their control in Africa also sparked a number of civil wars and other conflicts, yet European propaganda depicted what they were doing in Africa as a type of civilizing mission.

There is little doubt that colonization did a great deal to fuel ethnic tensions which would later lead to many internal conflicts within Africa, but we must also focus on the centuries of slave trading that went on in Africa because this event also caused chaos and destruction in Africa, and actually set the stage for Europe's later colonization of Africa. W.E.B. Du Bois raises the following question:

> In these states and in later years in Benin the whole character of west-coast culture seems to change. In place of the Yoruban culture, with its city democracy, its elevated religious ideas, its finely organized industry, and its noble art, came Ashanti and

Dahomey. What was it that changed the character of the west coast from this to the orgies of war and blood sacrifice which we read of later in these lands?

Du Bois concluded that the answer is "the slave trade." He continues, "the sale of men, but an organized traffic of such proportions and widely organized ramifications as to turn the attention and energies of men from nearly all other industries, encourage war and all the cruelest passions of way [...]."

To digress for a moment, I should address the claims of savagery in Dahomey and Asante (also known as Ashanti) because we often hear tales of African savagery, but it is also important to look at the other side of these supposed savage African states. Between the two previously mentioned states, Dahomey was the more militarized and authoritarian state—Dahomey was referred to as the "Black Sparta" for its military organization. Dahomey's military is most known for its army of women soldiers; popularly known as the Amazons of Dahomey. These women were feared for their ferocity and skill.

For all the tales of Dahomey's savagery (including human sacrifices) there are other aspects of Dahomey that need to be addressed. For example, Dahomey conducted a population census and established a system of espionage. Dahomey also produced artwork. This included wall paintings, sculptures, and cloth. The level of development in Dahomey was far from primitive savagery. Like most African societies, Dahomey was also very communal and family-oriented. For example, it was a traditional practice in Dahomey that a son-in-law would join a work group to perform tasks for the father of his wife.

The savagery of the Asante kingdom was also exaggerated. The Asante people had demonstrated the capacity for innovations outside of warfare. They had developed kente cloth by taking imported silk, unraveling it, and then combining the silk threads with cotton. The savagery of these kingdoms is also exaggerated in regards to human sacrifices. In "Human Sacrifice in Pre-Colonial

21

West Africa," Robin Law writes:

> Detailed studies of the background to the French expedition against Dahomey in 1892 and the British expeditions against Asante in 1896 and Benin in 1897, for example, have demonstrated how grossly exaggerated reports of human sacrifices in these societies were employed to justify the use of military force against them.

So how did the slave trade change African societies for the worse? One explanation that can be given was that the rewards for selling slaves to the Europeans served to increase the amount of warfare in Africa because Africans would engage in warfare to obtain those slaves. Pro-slavery propaganda typically stated that the war captives who were sold into slavery were captured in wars that were unrelated to the slave trade itself, but Thomas Watt visited Timbo, in Fouta Djallon, where he was told by one of the leaders "that the sole object of their wars was to procure slaves, as they could not obtain European goods without slaves, and they could not get slaves without fighting for them." John Newton (a former slave trader, who later became an abolitionist and author of "Amazing Grace") believed that the greater portion of wars in Africa would have ceased if the Europeans stopped tempting the Africans with goods in return for the slaves. Alexander Falconbridge, a doctor who worked onboard the slave ships, mentions how peace was restored in Angola during a period in which the slave trade was temporarily suspended. He writes:

> The failure of the trade for that period, as far as we could learn, had no other effect than to restore peace and confidence among the natives, which, upon the arrival of ships, is immediately destroyed by the inducement then held forth in the purchase of slaves.

The Europeans portrayed the slave trade as a civilizing mission, when it was in fact creating more violence and warfare in Africa. The slave trade also changed the nature of these wars. Despite the fact that Africans engaged in internal wars among each other, Ray

Kea pointed out that these wars were "limited to comparatively small-scale offensive operations, embracing tens rather than hundreds of square miles."

In 1602, De Marees pointed out: "The wars do not last long; they are started with great speed and also quickly ended." Muller observed a few cases in which "the enemy, having obtained the upper hand, practiced great violence, stealing, plundering, burning house," but he also notes that this happened "very seldom, since they are usually content with a hard fight, especially when they notice that one of the parties in dispute is a match for the other." Muller continues: "This is why a war for which people have prepared for such a long period comes to an end in two or three days."

One of the ways European presence increased the presence of wars in Africa was by intensifying existing rivalries between Africans or by setting one group off against another. In the region that would later become Guinea-Bissau, there were more than a dozen ethnic groups and the Europeans found that it was so easy to create conflicts between them that this area was known as a slave trader's paradise. Anne Bailey points out that Europeans often armed Africans whenever it suited their purposes, which "only served to fan the flames of preexisting conflicts and to create new ones where they would not otherwise have existed." It was certainly the case that Africans did engage in internal wars and the captives of those wars were usually taken into servitude, but with the rise of the Atlantic Slave Trade the frequency and destructive nature of wars in Africa increased. John Coleman De Graft-Johnson explained that Europeans "manufactured quarrels among tribesmen and set them at each other's throats, taking care, of course, to supply them with modern weapons."

John Atkins wrote that in the part of West Africa that he was in that the inhabitants "never care to walk even a mile from home without firearms," which illustrates the type of fear and insecurity that Africans lived in during the slave trade. Mama Dzagba, a Queen Mother in Eweland, recalled that during the slave trade "one man alone was not allowed to go single." There was the ever-present fear of being kidnapped and taken into slavery.

Graft-Johnson gives the following description of Africa prior to the slave trade: "Traders travelled hundreds and sometimes thousands of miles from one side of the vast continent to the other without molestation, for the stranger was always an honoured guest to the African. The tribal wars from which the European pirates claimed to deliver the people were mere sham-fights; it was a great battle when half a dozen men perished on a battlefield."

The slave trade also changed the system of punishment in Africa. Being sold into slavery became a frequent occurrence for those who had committed a crime. The customary laws which governed African societies were gradually changed by the slave trade, in ways that were beneficial for the slave traders. Just about every offence, no matter how trivial it may have seemed, carried with it the punishment of being sold into slavery. For example, in 1570 a man was climbing a palm tree and fell. The fall resulted in his death. The king's officials immediately seized the man's family and sold them into slavery. Falling from a palm tree actually became a crime, and the punishment for such a crime would be that the deceased's family would be sold into slavery. In 1822, Major Laing traveled to a section of Temne territory where the slave trade had been stamped out. He witnessed the interrogation of a girl who had died. The verdict was that no one was responsible for her death, but Major Laing pointed out that "had the slave trade existed, some unfortunate individual might have been accused and sold into captivity." Robert Campbell noted that in the city of Abeokuta the punishment for theft was "either decapitation or foreign slavery."

The Ewe people had a tradition for punishing offenders that was known as the Nyiko. If someone in the community had committed an offense—such as theft, adultery, or becoming pregnant out of wedlock—they would be brought to a trial and if found guilty they would be executed. During the period of the slave trade those who were found to be guilty under the Nyiko custom were simply sold to the Europeans. Rodney explained that the deprivation of liberty as a legal penalty for a crime in the Upper Guinea coast "makes its appearance in the seventeenth century when the process of law had become warped under the pressure of the Atlantic slave-trade, and there was hardly an offence which did not carry the penalty of sale into the hands of the Europeans."

Apologists for the European involvement in the slave trade often point to the fact that slavery was already practiced in Africa prior to the Europeans arriving there. The general narrative of this claim is that the Europeans merely continued the slave trade that had already existed in Africa before they arrived there, but we find that what was termed "slavery" in Africa could scarcely be compared to the slave system that was to be established in the Americas. Martin Delany had to say of slavery in Africa:

> It is simply preposterous to talk about slavery, as that term is understood, either being legalized or existing in this part of Africa. It is nonsense. The system is a patriarchal one, there being no actual difference, socially, between the slave (called by their protector *son or daughter*) and the children of the person with whom they live. Such persons intermarry, and frequently become the heads of state: indeed, generally so, as I do not remember at present a king or chief with whom I became acquainted whose entire members of the household, from the lowest domestic to the highest official, did not sustain this relation to him, they calling him *baba* or "father," and he treating them as children. And where this is not the case, it either arises from some innovation among them or those exceptional cases of despotism to be found in every country. Indeed, the term "slave" is unknown to them, only as it has been introduced among them by whites from Europe and America. So far from abject slavery, not even the old feudal system, as known to exist until comparatively recent in enlightened and Christian Europe, exists in this part of Africa.

The practice of treating captive persons as family was common throughout Africa. Among the Latuka people in Uganda there was a practice of capturing children and women during wars.

25

Cunningham gave this description of that practice under the rule of Queen Tofain:

> In the days when intertribal wars prevailed, her warriors were noted for bravery and discipline. They received no pay, but were allowed to retain all the children and women captured in the enemy's country, the captives becoming part of the household of the warrior who took them prisoners; they were not treated as slaves, but became an integral part of the warrior's family.

The Gold Coast born lawyer Joseph Casely Hayford gave his take on slavery in Africa, explaining:

> Gold Coast slavery was neither the slavery of ancient Rome, nor that of Afro-American history. The Gold Coast master was always humane and considerate. He actually went so far as to consider the slave a member of his family, and to adopt him as such.

Olaudah Equiano, whose father had a number of slaves, describes the difference as follows:

> Those prisoners which were not sold or redeemed, we kept as slaves: but how different was their condition from that of the slaves in the West Indies! With us, they do no more work than other members of the community, even their master; their food, clothing and lodging were nearly the same as theirs, (except that they were not permitted to eat with those who were free-born;) and there was scarce any other difference between them, than a superior degree of importance which the head of a family possesses in our state, and that authority which, as such, he exercises over every part of his household. Some of these slaves have even slaves under them as their own property, and for their own use.

The system of slavery that Equiano became a victim of in the West

Indies was very much different from the system of servitude and slavery that he was familiar with in his homeland. Equiano recorded that slaves were tortured with devices such as chains, iron muzzles and thumbscrews. The conditions that the slaves were transported in were horrendous. Equiano recalled that the smell was so bad that they could not eat. The situation that Equiano was in was so terrible that he found himself wishing for his "former slavery."

Mungo Park gave the following description of slavery based on his experiences in West Africa:

> They [the slaves] claim no reward for their services, except food and clothing; and are treated with kindness or severity, according to the good or bad disposition of their masters. Custom, however, has established certain rules with regard to the treatment of slaves, which it is thought dishonourable to violate. Thus the domestic slaves, or such as are born in a man's own house, are treated with more lenity than those which are purchased with money. The authority of the master over the domestic slave, as I have elsewhere observed, extends only to reasonable correction; for the master cannot sell his domestic, without having first brought him to a public trial before the chief men of the place.

Such restrictions on the master were not extended to those who were either bought or captured as prisoners of war. Park noted that it was common practice for people to be taken as slaves during a war. He wrote of an instance in which the King of Bambarra went to war with Kaarta. In the first day of conflict, the King of Bambarra took 900 prisoners. Park observed that there were two kinds of wars that were practiced in Africa. The first of which was known as *killi* or "to call out." It was called this "because such wars are openly avowed, and previously declared." Park explains: "Wars of this description in Africa commonly terminate, however, in the course of a single campaign. A battle is fought; the vanquished seldom think of rallying again; the whole inhabitants become panic-struck, and the conquerors have only to bind the slaves, and carry off their plunder and their victims. Such of the prisoners as, through age or infirmity, are unable to endure fatigue, or are found unfit for sale, are considered as useless, and I have no doubt are frequently put to death. The same fate commonly awaits a chief, or any other person who has taken a very distinguished part in the war."

This form of warfare resulted in a large number of prisoners of war, who became slaves. Park wrote that such conflicts typically lasted a single campaign, therefore they were relatively shorter and less destructive than the wars that were fought in Europe. Park himself noted that *killi* was the form of warfare in Africa that bore the greatest resemblance to European wars. The other form of war was *tegria* or "plundering or stealing." This form of warfare was conducted in secret, with no notice of attack being given.

Park concluded:

> When a Negro has, by means like these, once fallen into the hands of his enemies, he is either retained as the slave of his conqueror, or bartered into a distant kingdom; for an African, when he has once subdued his enemy, will seldom give him an opportunity of lifting up his hand against him at a future period. A conqueror commonly disposes of his captives according to the rank which they held in their native kingdom. Such of the domestic slaves as appear to be of a mild disposition, and particularly the young women, are retained as his own slaves. Others that display marks of discontent are disposed of in a distant country; and such of the freemen or slaves, as have taken an active part in the war, are either sold to the Slatees or put to death. War, therefore, is certainly the most general and most productive source of slavery; and the desolations of war often (but not always) produce the second cause of slavery, *famine*; in which case a freeman becomes a slave to avoid a greater calamity.

Park's description of slavery in Africa was certainly much different than that which existed in the Americas. Those who were enslaved through being captured in war were generally treated worse, but these were not people who were born into a perpetual system of chattel slavery as African people in the Americas were. The laws in African societies concerning slavery sometimes made European slave traders impatient because they were not being supplied with the amount of slaves that they wanted. In the Kongo, only criminals and prisoners of war were allowed to be sold into slavery. This meant that Affonso, the king of the Kongo, could only supply a relatively small number of slaves, and the Portuguese slavers began encouraging crime and instigated wars in the Kongo in order to acquire more slaves.

During his travels in Africa, Robert Campbell also gave his impression of slavery:

> Although the term "slavery" is the only word by which the institution can be properly designated, it is certainly not of the same character as the American institution, there being but little disparity between the condition of the master and that of his slave, since the one possesses almost every advantage accessible to the other. Slaves are often found filling the most exalted positions: thus at Abbeokuta all the king's chief officers are his slaves, and they are among his most confidential advisers. On certain state occasions, one or other of these slaves is often permitted to assume in public the position of the king, and command and receive in his own person the homage and respect due to his master.

Slaves were obtained mainly through conquest. Campbell explained that some of these wars were "justifiable", while others were undertaken solely to acquire slaves. Others became slaves as a penalty for committing a crime. Some of these slaves were sold to pay either their own debts or the debts of others. Children were sometimes also kidnapped and sold as slaves. In the Muslim kingdom of Ilorin, Campbell found a large slave market. In Ilorin, Campbell traveled with Nasamo, the king's sheriff. Despite his high position, Nasamo was himself a slave who was stolen from his home in his youth—this demonstrates how in Africa enslaved persons could rise to high ranking positions that could never be attained by enslaved Africans in the United States. Campbell spoke with Nasamo about the evils of slavery, which Nasamo agreed. Nasamo wished that there was no slavery, but he also felt that it was better to have exposed slave markets "for then bad men would seize the defenseless and our children, and we would not know where to find them." Campbell observed that the Muslims never sold other Muslims into slavery. They sometimes held Muslims as slaves, but only when the person was purchased as a non-Muslim and then converted.

Wilfrid D. Hambly records that among the Ovimbundu if one is unable to pay their debts then their sister's children would be taken as domestic slaves. The children are set free when the debt is finally paid. Hambly explains that "these domestic slaves were not ill treated, though their rights were limited." Under this system the slave held no property and was not allowed to buy their freedom. In cases where slaves ran away, they would be tracked down with dogs. The slave also had the ability to appeal to the headman if they were treated cruelly by their master.

In the Asante and Dahomey kingdoms, slaves were given better treatment than slaves in the Americas and had significantly more freedoms. In the first place, slavery or servitude in these two kingdoms had varying degrees based on how one came to become a servant. One could become a slave through being kidnapped, as a form of punishment for certain offences, or being sold into slavery by a relative, parent, or chieftain. Some people often sold themselves into slavery for several reasons. Among the reasons included financial hardships, especially during periods of famine. Slavery provided a means of obtaining economic security for some. For this reason King Gezo argued that it would be impossible to abolish slavery in Dahomey due to the negative backlash that it would create. Not only would it have affected all of his headmen and officers, but it would leave many slaves homeless and destitute.

War captives were also forced into servitude, which was significant given the warlike nature of both kingdoms. In Dahomey, war captives were used to replace whatever men Dahomey lost during their battles. Children born of domestic slaves were automatically considered citizens of Dahomey and had all the rights of the average Dahomean citizen. Likewise, the Asante also incorporated slaves into their military. Slaves were also used as human sacrifices in religious ceremonies in Asante and Dahomey.

In many West African societies there was a tradition of burying servants, friends, and family members of a deceased ruler along with that ruler so that they could attend to the ruler in the afterlife. Arab travelers in the Ghana Kingdom noted the practice of burying royal servants along with the deceased king. This was yet another aspect of African society that the slave trade had altered. European observers noted an increase in human sacrifices in West Africa during the eighteenth and nineteenth centuries. In Dahomey, for example, human sacrifice was practiced at an unprecedented rate in comparison to states such as Allada and Whydah. The increase of human sacrifices was a result of the increasing militarization of West African states, which was a byproduct of the slave trade. Mary Kingsley noted that early European travelers to Benin made no mention of human sacrifice in Benin, although mentions of human sacrifice appeared in the accounts of more recent travelers to Benin. Kingsley herself believed that the "custom of sacrificing human beings has been steadily increasing of late years" in Benin.

King Agaja is said to have started the tradition of "Annual Customs" in which human sacrifices were made in tribute to the deceased kings of Dahomey. Those who were sacrificed were typically criminals and war captives. Aside from paying tribute to the former kings of Dahomey, King Kpengla explained that this annual custom was used to instill fear among the enemies of Dahomey. The Asante Kingdom also developed a tradition of conducting massive human sacrifices during annual ceremonies.

This included offering human sacrifices to the gods to ensure successful military expeditions.

Boniface Obichere writes that the Trans-Atlantic slave trade "increased the number of slaves in these two kingdoms." It also created a class of people who specialized in slave dealing and professional kidnappers, although the security in Dahomey made kidnapping a rare occurrence. The slave trade in effect made slave trading a business in Asante and Dahomey. Another change in society that it created was that, in the words of Obichere, it "tended to destroy the humane treatment of slaves in Asante and Dahomey."

Yet another aspect of slavery in West Africa is that it seems to have been non-existent in some areas. Walter Rodney notes that "one is struck by the absence of references to local African slavery in the sixteenth or even the seventeenth century [...]." He further writes that "one can identify no African slavery, serfdom or the like on the Upper Guinea Coast during the first phase of European contact [...]." What he is indicating here is that slavery in this section of Africa (the Upper Guinea Coast) was seemingly non-existent until the arrival of the Europeans who built entire colonies that were dependent on slave labor.

Indeed, if slavery was so prevalent in the Upper Guinea Coast of Africa, the Portuguese certainly made little mention of it, though they gave detailed accounts of various other aspects of African life. In fact, the only instance in which labor services were linked to limited privileges in the Upper Guinea Coast was in Sierra Leone at the beginning of the 17th century. If a subject was in danger in one kingdom, he could flee to another kingdom where he would be at the mercy of the king. He was the king's slave and could be sold to the Europeans. Valentim Fernandes stated: "The king has no servants other than his slaves. Sometimes a young stranger arrives and seeks the protection of the king, who looks upon the young man as his own." Fernandes noted that Wolof nobles had households that consisted of a wife, children, and slaves. The slaves worked six days a week for the wife and one day a week for themselves.

Evidence would suggest that domestic slavery in Africa actually increased as a result of the slave trade. As Anne Bailey argued,

"Atlantic operations greatly increased and influenced the maintenance and growth of domestic slavery." Bailey also writes about a specific domestic slavery practice known as trokosi. In this tradition, young women are forced to serve priests in order to atone for a debt or for an offense that was committed by her family. Many of these women are sexually abused by the priests. Bailey argues that the custom of trokosi is part of the legacy of the slave trade.

The practice of domestic slavery that developed in West Africa was often times a very brutal one. Mary Kingsley noted a specific instance in which an "old and powerful chief" became extremely jealous towards his slave. This young slave was looked upon with "too much favour" by the chief's young wife. He became furiously jealous, which resulted in this chief shooting his slave in the head with a revolver and then having the body dumped into a river. This type of behavior was not necessarily the norm, as Kingsley explained, but it demonstrated the absolute power that masters wielded over their slaves:

> I do not wish to convey to my readers the idea that all chiefs in the Niger Delta are cruel monsters, but they all have power of life and death over their slaves; the mildest of them occasionally may find themselves so placed that they are compelled in conformity with some Ju-Ju right to sacrifice a slave or two. The ordinary punishments for theft and insubordination practised amongst these people are often terribly cruel and unnecessarily severe.

Kingsley's description of the kingdom of Bonny provides more insight into how the slave trade impacted the social development of African kingdoms. Kingsley explained that the people of Bonny "were the greatest slave traders in Western Africa" and she notes that on average 16,000 people a year were brought out of Bonny to be sold into slavery—Kingsley herself notes that these numbers do not include the numbers of those who died during the journey to the coast or those who were executed after being rejected for sale by the European buyers. After the abolition of the slave trade, Bonny turned to trading palm oil as a source of commerce. The slave trade had such a marked impact on Bonny that Kingsley explained there were more slaves than freemen in Bonny and a person who was born to slave parents in Bonny was regarded as being equal to freemen.

Bonny, in many ways, also reflected the harsh nature of African society during the epoch of the slave trade. For instance, for a man to be made a chief in Bonny he had to cut off the head of another man in war. Alternatively, a man could also fulfill this head-cutting requirement by purchasing a slave and then beheading that slave. No man could become a chief without partaking in this ceremony. In some cases, men who fit the requirement to become a chief declined to participate in the head-cutting and had to be forced to do so. Bonny was also among the African societies in which twins were executed.

Jaja, who had been a slave in Bonny, was elected as a chief. Jaja was eventually forced to leave Bonny. He established a kingdom of his own, known as Opobo. Jaja's accomplishments as a statesman and trader are remarkable when one considers the circumstances that Jaja came from. Mr. H. H. Johnston stated that Jaja "was cut out by nature for a king, and he has the instinct of rule, though it not unfrequently degenerates into cruel tyranny." Indeed, Jaja could at times be cruel, although the circumstances that confronted him justified some of this cruelty. For example, Jaja was known to have conducted raids against the Kwo Ibo people, destroying their villages and taking the inhabitants as prisoners. Kingsley explained that these raids by Jaja "were to a great extent brought on by the actions of the Ibrons themselves, who were not slow to attack and slay any Opobo men they caught wandering about, if the latter were not in sufficient numbers to defend themselves." Opobo also retained the head-cutting requirement for a man to become a chief.

The decision to begin the slave trade was not a decision made by both parties. The Africans and Europeans did not sit down to work out a deal, and initially this was not even a slave trade. Europeans did not originally go to Africa in search of slaves. They originally went to Africa in search of gold and trade. The Portuguese traded gold on the coast of Africa. In the early part of the 1440s the Portuguese obtained and brought back some African slaves. The Portuguese would then conduct a series of slave raids along the coast of Africa. The first major slave raid took place in 1444, led by Lançarote de Freitas.

This method of acquiring slaves proved to be dangerous, however. The slave trader Nuno Tristão was killed during a battle with some native Africans that he intended to enslave. This also challenges the assertion that Europeans did not physically steal any Africans. It was not the norm, but there were cases of Europeans raiding villages to get African slaves. John Hawkins was another notorious slave raider. He made three voyages to Africa in which he stole Africans and sold them for profit. Hawkins would later be knighted by the Queen for his actions.

The slave raid of Captain Smith is yet another example of raiding for slaves. In Massachusetts the laws concerning slavery were that slaves could only be obtained if they were captured in a just war or if they sold themselves into slavery. In 1640, Captain Smith attacked an African village and brought back some Africans. He was arrested and the slaves were returned home. Eventually, however, slave trading would come to be viewed as legitimate commerce in Massachusetts.

Some have sought to portray the relationship between the Europeans and the Africans as an equal partnership, but this was not the case. Europe benefited more from this so-called trade than Africans did. While the Europeans were able to build wealthy industries off of the backs of the African slaves, in return for these slaves Africans received items such as cheap gunpowder, gin, rum, glass beads, and other junk—things that were otherwise unsellable or useless in Europe. We also must keep in mind that following the end of the slave trade, many of these same African kings who had traded with the Europeans would come to be overthrown and exiled by the Europeans.

This is not to deny that Africans did play a major role in the slave trade, but we must keep in mind that it was European desires that began the Trans-Atlantic slave trade and made it the large industry that it became. Walter Rodney sums this up when he states:

> When the European powers involved in the area (namely Britain, France and Portugal) intervened to end slavery and serfdom in their respective colonies, they were simply undoing their own handiwork.

Another aspect of the slave trade is that there has been a conscious attempt to shift an equal amount of the blame (and in some cases a greater amount) on the part of the Africans. The author of a book titled *Sins of Our Father* admitted that many white people had urged him to state that the slave trade was solely the responsibility of the Africans. Scholars like Henry Louis Gates contribute to the misunderstanding of the African role in the slave trade by not revealing the full story.

Gates wrote an article called "Ending the Slavery Blame-Game," in which he attempts to complicate the discussion over reparations by explaining the African role in the slave trade, but what Gates ends up doing is further propagating European whitewashing of history. In his article Gates mentions four kingdoms that were involved in the slave trade: Asante, Dahomey, Kongo, and Ndongo. It is true that all four of these kingdoms were involved in the slave trade in one way or another, but in all four kingdoms are examples of African rulers who actively resisted the slave trade and European imperialism.

King Affonso I of the Kongo Kingdom tried to establish ties with the Portuguese. He willingly converted to Christianity and learned how to read and write in Portuguese—one of the priests wrote that Affonso knew the prophets and the Gospel better than they did. He also expressed a desire for the Portuguese to send priests, doctors, and other specialists because he eagerly wanted his people to learn from the Portuguese. Instead, the Portuguese sent slavers to acquire more slaves. Affonso was initially involved in the slave trade. He sold his captives as slaves, but the Portuguese greed for slaves became too overwhelming. The

Portuguese began kidnapping and enslaving free Africans. Affonso wrote a series of letters to the Portuguese king (King Joao II) pleading to stop the practice of stealing freed subjects and enslaving them.

Affonso wrote: "Each day the traders are kidnapping our people—children of this country, sons of our nobles and vassals, even people of our own family...This corruption and depravity are so widespread that our land is entirely depopulated..." Affonso further writes: "It is our wish that this kingdom not be a place for the trade or transport of slaves."

Affonso also noted that the greed of his people drove them to seize members of their own families and sell them into slavery. The slave trade had gotten out of the control of King Affonso and he desperately wanted an end to it. The Portuguese paid little attention to Affonso's request and continued their trade of African slaves, however. In 1539 King Affonso found out that 10 of his relatives, including nephews and grandchildren, had disappeared en route to Portugal. They would become slaves in Brazil. Affonso's opposition to the slave trade did not go over well with some of the Portuguese traders. In 1540 some Portuguese merchants made an attempt to assassinate King Affonso, but it failed.

The growing slave activity in the Kongo had caused the decline of the once powerful kingdom. According to tradition the founding king of the Kongo was named Nimi a Lukeni. Nimi's father was Nimi a Nzima. Nimi a Lukeni established himself at a ferry on the Kwangu (or Kwango) river and levied a toll on all those who crossed the river. As the story goes, one day Lukeni's aunt attempted to cross the stream. She claimed exemption from paying the toll because she was the sister of the chief, who was Lukeni's father. Lukeni responded by having his aunt killed. The members of the clan protected Lukeni from his father's wrath. Lukeni then installed himself as the king. Lukeni expanded the Kongo Kingdom through conquest.

The Kongo expanded through military conquests and was

largely maintained through military force. At times provinces attempted to break away from the kingdom. There were also occasional revolts against taxation, although the benefits of trade and the military power of the Kongo Kingdom typically discouraged rebellion. David Lopes gave the following description of the governmental structure of the Kongo Kingdom:

> From his throne of ivory and sculpted wood, the king ruled through an elaborate network of councilors and governors, clan elders and local chieftains, priests and electors. He maintained that network through alliance, marriage, trade, and force. Of his 12 councilors, four by statute were women. In theory, the king could neither declare war nor open a road without the councilors' consent; in practice, the king's power depended on his political skills. A strong king, for example, could replace his governors at will; a weak one struggled to maintain their loyalty. No rule of primogeniture applied. Instead, clan elders picked the future king from among the sons of the dying king's lesser wives. Despite the fact that successions were sometimes bloody, it was a system that ensured continuity: anyone sharp enough to earn the clan elders' loyalty was usually savvy enough to rule.

The women in the royal family of the Kongo Kingdom exercised significant political influence as well. In 1531, the king of Portugal sent a series of letters to important people in the Kongo. One of these letters was directed to "the daughter and mother of a king" who by custom "commands in everything in Congo." The wife of the king was also an administrative official in the kingdom. In 1513, Affonso departed for a campaign in the south. He left a Portuguese man named Alvaro Lopes in charge of the capital. Under Lopes' watch there was a slave revolt in which several people were killed. Lopes did not want to punish the slaves too severely because they belonged to the vicar of the Kongo, so he ordered that they be whipped, but Affonso's wife intervened and ordered that the slaves be killed because the custom in the Kongo was "that those who kill are killed", so Lopes ordered the slaves killed instead.

Located to the north of the Kongo Kingdom was the Loango Kingdom. The people of the Loango Kingdom spoke the same Kikongo language that was spoken in the Kongo Kingdom. Andrew Battell described the capital town of the Loango Kingdom as being a town where the houses were built under palm and plantain trees. He also notes: "The streets are wide and long, and always clean swept. The King hath his houses on the west side, and before his door he hath a plain, where he sitteth, when he has any feastings or matters of wars to treat of." According to Battell, the king of Loango had ten houses.

The previous ruler, Njimbe, never spoke during the day, but Battell observed that the new king spoke during the day. The king was also never to be seen eating or drinking. Whenever the king was drinking, those who were present were made to look away. Those who failed to do so were executed. The king was the supreme ruler. Battell noted that the people viewed the king as a sort of god who had the power to make rain. The king also maintained his authority through a group of people known as *Dondos*. These were albinos who were presented to the king when they were born. These children became the "king's witches" and they were considered so powerful that no one dared to meddle with them. The king himself was viewed as a witch.

Despite the supernatural abilities that were ascribed to the ruling king, the Kingdom of Loango was a decentralized kingdom. Battell explained that Loango was governed by four princes who were all the sons of the king's sisters. Succession to the throne was matrilineal, which meant that the king's own sons could never become king. It was one of the sons of the king's sisters who succeeded the king whenever he died. The mother of the princes also had an important role. Battell described her as being "the highest and chief woman in all the land."

The Europeans first made contact with the Kongo Kingdom in 1482 when Diogo Cão led an expedition into the Kongo. The Portuguese would eventually establish communication with the

Kongo. The first ruler to embrace Christianity in the Kongo took the name of João. João's wife Leonor Nzinga a Nlaza also displayed an interest in Christianity and she demanded to be baptized as well. When João died there was a civil war in which Dom Affonso emerged victorious. Affonso was succeeded by Dom Pedro. It was during the reign of Dom Pedro that the first bishop for the Kongo was appointed by Rome. Pedro was himself educated in Portugal. Pedro's reign was a short one and he was succeeded by his brother Dom Francisco. Dom Francisco also died after a short reign and he was succeeded by Dom Diego. Dom Diego was remembered as a very intelligent and noble ruler who was also a great warrior who conquered many neighboring states.

Diego died around 1561. Shortly after this the Portuguese decided to intervene in the affairs of the Kongo by instigating the assassination of a popular candidate for the throne. Affonso II ascended to the throne, but was assassinated by his brother Bernardo, who was supported by the Portuguese. This caused the people of the Kongo to revolt against the Portuguese, killing many of them including the priests. After Bernardo's death, he was succeeded by Dom Henrique. Henrique's reign was a short one. He died from a wound that he received in battle and was succeeded by Alvaro I.

Alvaro sent an embassy to Portugal to apologize for the previously mentioned killings of the Portuguese in the Kongo. In 1568 the Kongo was devastated by an attack from the Jaga people. The devastation was so great that many died of hunger. Others were forced to sell their family members to obtain food. Many were also carried away by the Portuguese to be sold into slavery. The king of the Kongo was so overwhelmed that he requested the assistance of the Portuguese. With the help of the Portuguese the Jaga people were finally driven away.

The Kongo began to recover from the devastation brought forward by the Jaga people, but the Kongo remained a source of slaves. The European slave trading activity eventually altered the balance of power in the region. As the Portuguese distributed guns in the region, power shifted away from the capital and towards the provinces. Eventually Sonyo and other provinces declared their independence from the Kongo. There were also battles for secession which greatly weakened the Kongo's power. Eight kings ruled between 1614 and 1641. Among the rulers during this period was Dom Bernardo II, who was killed by his brother.

The Kongo was finally destroyed in 1665 after a war with the Portuguese. In the conflict over 5,000 soldiers from the Kongo were killed, including the ruling king at the time, Dom Antonio I. After this the Kongo fell into disarray. The kingdom splintered into competing chiefdoms who all claimed to be the legitimate successors to the throne. All of these rival chiefs were also dependent on the slave trade for their survival. The constant wars and the slave trade created a state of near anarchy in the Kongo. The situation in the Kongo was so terrible that one writer of the Kong's history was left to conclude: "And if we ask to what extent, and in what manner, have the natives of Kongo been benefited by two centuries of contact with the civilization of Europe, and of missionary effort, we feel bound to admit that they have not been benefited at all—either materially or morally."

Other kingdoms in the region would suffer similar fates. Ndongo was conquered by the Portuguese in 1671, with the Portuguese killing the ruler of the kingdom and enslaving his followers. In 1680 Kanini took power in the Matamba kingdom. The Portuguese recognized that Kanini's efforts to expand his kingdom was detrimental to their own slave trading interests in the region so they sent an expedition against him, which he successfully repelled. In time, however, the Matamba Kingdom would be colonized by the Portuguese. The Kwanhama Kingdom was conquered by the Portuguese in 1915. In the scramble to colonize Africa, the remains of the Kongo Kingdom were divided among the French, Belgians, and Portuguese colonies of French Congo, Congo Free State, and Angola. The Loango Kingdom was also colonized, becoming part of the French Congo.

During this period of interaction between the Portuguese and the Kongo, the slave trade had devastated the Kongo and ultimately destroyed it. The Portuguese, on the other hand, benefitted from the slaves that it took from the Kongo. Gates

41

mentions that Antonio Manuel, who was an ambassador for the Kongo, went to Brazil to free someone who had wrongfully enslaved in Brazil, but he avoids elaborating on how the Portuguese slave traders destroyed the Kongo Kingdom. This was not an equal exchange or an equal partnership on both sides.

Dahomey's involvement in the slave trade is particularly notorious, especially during the reign of Gezo who was very reluctant to agree to the abolition of the slave trade. Prior to Gezo's rule, his brother Adandozan held the throne. Adandozan's rule saw a decline in the slave trade due to Adandozan's own lack of success in combat, which limited the number of war captives available to sell into slavery. One of the apparent reasons for Adandozan being deposed was that his lack of military success was not supplying enough war captives for sacrifice.

Adandozan found it difficult to work with the Portuguese because they were untrustworthy and misleading. For instance, he complained that Portuguese merchants used counterfeit money to buy captives. He also complained that the Portuguese changed the prices of captives. Adandozan had particular issues with a Portuguese slave trader named Francisco Felix de Sousa. Sousa eventually found himself being imprisoned by Adandozan. It is therefore no surprise that Sousa played a key role in the coup that overthrew Adandozan and brought Gezo into power. Afterwards, Gezo and de Sousa enjoyed a close partnership.

Gezo expanded the trade in captives beyond what Adandozan had done and it is believed that Gezo sold many of Adandozan's relatives and supporters into slavery. Gezo was such a staunch advocate of the slave trade that he had sent a letter to Queen Victoria requesting that Dahomey be granted a monopoly over the slave trade and also expressed his hope that the queen would send him guns "to make war."

Despite this infamous reputation, during Gezo's rule Dahomey underwent some important developments and many of the Europeans who encountered Gezo remarked favorably about him. For instance, T.B. Freeman and John Duncan described Gezo as having a pleasant personality and good manners. De Sousa depicted Gezo as a generous ruler, for when De Sousa requested that Adandozan give him 40 bags of cowries, Adandozan gave him

40 bags of corn instead, but Gezo gave De Sousa a bag of cowries. Gezo was also described as a remarkable husband and father, and was known for the way that he humbly spoke with his state officials and chiefs. Although the Europeans did not deny that Gezo was a despot, and a man who could at times be a tyrant, Gezo's character and administrative ability did not fail to impress many of the Europeans who visited the king. Although in theory the king of Dahomey held absolute power, he could not undertake any action without consulting his hierarchy of chiefs. This hierarchy included a Mingan (Prime Minister), a Minister of Finance, a commander-in-chief of the army, and a Captain of the Whites.

Gezo demonstrated a remarkable capacity as a statesman. When Gezo came to the throne, Dahomey's economy was in decline. By this point Dahomey's economy was reliant on the slave trade, which Gezo continued, but he shifted Dahomey's economy towards other pursuits. He introduced a system of cash crop farming. Aside from cash crop farming, Gezo also encouraged weaving and mining, which helped to turn the attention of his subjects away from warfare.

Gezo's position on the slave trade was a controversial one. He argued that he could not immediately end the slave trade in Dahomey due to the adverse impact that it would have on the kingdom, although the British wanted an immediate stop to the slave trade. For this reason, Gezo came to view the British as a potential obstacle to his own economic interests. When Consul Beecroft and Commander Forbes visited Gezo in 1850 he told them that he was not an enemy of the British, but he also warned them that this would change if they did not evacuate Abeokuta, the city that Gezo was planning to attack. For this attack, Gezo also created an alliance with King Kosoko of Lagos, who would attack Badagry. Gezo's goal was to destroy Abeokuta and Badagry because these cities provided bases for the missionaries. Gezo intended to drive out the missionaries in an attempt to restore the slave trade. The attack on Abeokuta was ultimately a failure, but it demonstrated the extent to which Gezo fought to maintain the slave trade.

As a leader, Gezo made the welfare of his subjects a priority, which challenges the often depicted image of the kings of Dahomey merely being cruel despots that indulged solely in warfare, slave raiding, and human sacrifices. In fact, Gezo introduced more humane elements to Dahomean laws and customs. He abolished both the death penalty for adultery and the practice of immolating slaves. Gezo's subjects were also apparently happy under his rule and he even earned the admiration of some of his enemies. After Gezo's death, Freeman described him as being "one of the most remarkable men of his age [...]."

Despite the fact that Dahomey became reliant on the slave trade, this was not always the case. King Agaja Trudo, who reigned in the 1700s, recognized that the European demand for slaves was harmful to Dahomey's development. He responded to this by attacking and burning European forts along the coast. He also attacked trade factories in Allada and Whydah. Agaja had his troops block the paths that led into the interior, which greatly reduced the number of slaves being exported.

The Europeans were unable to defeat Agaja, but Agaja was also unsuccessful in his attempt to pursue other means of business with the Europeans. He sent a spokesman to England to appeal to European craftsmen. One European who stayed at the court of Dahomey in the 1720s stated "if any tailor, carpenter, smith or any other sort of white man that is free be willing to come here, he will find very good encouragement." Agaja found no success in this, however, as the only means of business which the Europeans wished to pursue was slave trading.

Agaja's need for guns forced him to reach an agreement with the Europeans. A big factor in why Europeans were able to successfully obtain so many slaves was that they were the ones with the firearms and the Africans had to rely on them to obtain these firearms. This is why Adandozan did not receive the firearms factory that he requested. From the stories of Agaja, Adandozan, and Gezo we can see that Dahomey, although a major player in the slave trade, did not maintain an equal partnership with European slave traders. Dahomey was involved in the slave trade to the extent that it benefitted them economically and militarily. This meant that at times Dahomey was at odds with Europeans.

In Angola, Nzinga of the Ndongo and Matamba kingdoms fought a war in opposition to the Portuguese slave traders. The Portuguese were threatening the political power and sovereignty of the Africans, which led to a conflict between the slave traders and Nzinga. Gates mentions this, but he mentions Nzinga within the context of her being involved in the slave trade and he downplays the extent of Nzinga's war with the slave traders.

Chancellor Williams described Nzinga as "one of the bravest generals that ever commanded an army." This is apt description for a woman who put up some of the fiercest resistance against a European power during the period of the slave trade. Ndongo was founded by a wise and generous blacksmith who was named Angola. Angola came from the Kongo and founded the Ndongo Kingdom. Angola was succeeded by a wicked son who was later driven out of power by a subject that he had wronged who was named Kiluanji kia Samba. By the time that Nzinga came of age Ndongo had been at the center of many of the disputes that arose in the region due to the slave trade.

By the 1620s Ndongo and the Portuguese were at war and a peace conference was held in 1622 between the two forces. Nzinga, who was the sister of the king at the time, led a delegation to this conference. Even though the Portuguese refused to recognize Nzinga as an equal, Nzinga ensured that they did. At this peace conference the Portuguese governor decided not to provide a chair for Nzinga. Nzinga refused to stand before the governor, however, and instead her attendants rolled out a royal carpet and then one of them went down on all–fours and acted as Nzinga's seat. This was done to demonstrate to the Portuguese that Nzinga was their equal.

Nzinga's brother died the next year, in 1623. Following this Nzinga became the ruler of the Ndongo kingdom. The Portuguese claimed that Nzinga had poisoned her brother, who was named Ngola Mbande. This claim has been disputed by some historians.

As Chancellor Williams notes, Nzinga certainly had reason to resent her brother, since some sources indicate that her brother forcibly seized the throne from their father and killed all potential rivals, including his brother and Nzinga's son. Nzinga also had her brother's son killed in order to assume power for herself rather than ruling alongside her nephew as a regent until he was old enough to come to power. Given that her own son was killed by her brother, killing her nephew may have also been an act of revenge. Whatever the case may have been, Nzinga was now the ruler of Ndongo.

Once Nzinga became the sole ruler, she decided to "become a man". This included keeping several male concubines and forcing them to wear women's clothes. In doing so Nzinga reversed the typical gender norms of Ndongo society. Kings engaged in polygamous marriages, so Nzinga decided to practice polyandry. Polyandry was also practiced among women who had obtained positions of political power in Kongo as well. Nzinga's "husbands" were made to sleep among her maids in waiting and if they sexually touched any of the maids they were killed. Although Nzinga was a woman, she ruled Ndongo as a king and set a precedent for the future of her kingdom. Following her death, many other women ruled Matamba as well. This would include Barbara, who was Nzinga's sister.

Nzinga became a threat to Portuguese interests because she demanded that the Portuguese respect the terms of her treaty with them or face war. Not only did Nzinga have to confront the Portuguese, but she also had to contend with internal rivals who sided with the Portuguese in an attempt to oust her from power. In 1621 the Portuguese had attempted to install a puppet ruler named Samba a Ntumba, but he was rejected because he did not descend from the royal family. The Portuguese also assisted Hari a Kiluanji in his attempt to wrestle power away from Nzinga.

The Portuguese had briefly succeeded in their attempt to install Kiluanji as king when in July 1626 they managed to drive Nzinga out of Angola. Nzinga returned in November 1627 and retook control of Ndongo. The Portuguese regrouped and were prepared for an all-out war against Nzinga. Rather than confront them in battle, Nzinga decided to outwit her enemies by putting out a rumor that she fled her country and was killed in enemy territory. Nzinga returned in 1629 and caught the Portuguese by surprise. By this time Nzinga had become the ruler of Matamba as well and in retaking Ndongo she became the ruler of two kingdoms.

In order to retain her position of power Nzinga was often forced to make pragmatic alliances. She aligned herself with the Imbangala people (sometimes referred to as Jaga as well). The Jaga people developed a very fearsome reputation for their warlike and cruel nature. Chancellor Williams described them as being "a roaming tribe that seemed to be more interested in raids of destruction than in settling anywhere." The Europeans also generally believed the Jaga people to have been cannibals. Andrew Battell spent some time among the Jaga people. He described them as a nomadic people who frequently raided other countries. He also noted that they had a peculiar tradition of infanticide in which newborn babies were buried alive after they were born. Battell explained that "when they take any town they keep the boys and girls of thirteen or fourteen years of age as their own children. But the men and women they kill and eat." The boys were trained to be warriors. Battell also observed a tradition of human sacrifice among the Jaga people as well.

The Imbangala armies supported Nzinga, although this was an uneasy alliance and in 1628 the Imbangala decided to change sides during a battle. Nzinga decided to become an Imbangala herself. She not only adopted their customs, but she promised to marry the Imbangala chief Kasanji. During this period Nzinga's army also adopted the tactics that were used by the Imbangala people. This was not a permanent alliance, however. Nzinga had been baptized in 1622 and she returned to Christianity again in the 1640s in an attempt to oust the Imbangala influence. In doing so Nzinga also repudiated the practices of the Imbangala, such a cannibalism and infanticide. Nzinga claimed that she had been driven to join the Imbangala due to extreme circumstances.

Nzinga established herself as a fierce warrior who personally led her troops into battle. Her opposition to the Portuguese proved to be the greatest threat to Portuguese interests in Africa, as the following passage points out:

> Who ever heard of a woman general, leading her armies in person? The truth is that she is the greatest military strategist that ever confronted the armed forces of Portugal. Her tactics keep our commanders sweating in confusion and dismay. Her aim is nothing less than the total destruction of the slave trade. To this end—and what alarms us most—she has developed a system of infiltrating our Black troops with her own men, causing whole companies to rebel, desert, and join her armies in what she calls a 'War of Liberation. . . .' Portuguese casualties are always heavier than reported, for she stages surprise attacks with lightning speed, always aiming first to capture guns and cannons.

In her effort to combat the Portuguese slave traders, Nzinga made her state a haven for runaways who had escaped their slavers. Many of these runaways joined Nzinga's army. Along with adding these runaways to her ranks, Nzinga was able to win over many of Portugal's African allies to her cause. Despite her opposition to the enslavement of her own people, Nzinga sold enemy chiefs and their followers into slavery. Chancellor Williams explained that "Nzinga was particularly ruthless with captured Black chiefs who were allies of the whites. She did not hesitate to sell such chiefs and their followers into slavery." Henry Louis Gates noted that Nzinga also "sold African traditional religious leaders into slavery, claiming they had violated her new Christian precepts." Nzinga had also traded two hundred slaves to secure the freedom of her sister Barbara, who had been captured by the Portuguese.

The Dutch eventually withdrew and ended the alliance. Portugal gained the upper hand in 1648 when they managed to isolate Matamba. This tactic proved successful as Nzinga was forced to resume business with the Portuguese, signing a treaty with them in 1656 after having engaged them in combat for nearly four decades. Walter Rodney explained that once "trade in slaves had been started in any given part of Africa, it soon became clear that it was beyond the capacity of any single African state to change the situation." Nzinga did attempt some resistance against the Portuguese slave traders, but in the end, she was forced to continue slave trading with them.

Gates also neglects to mention the near 100 year conflict fought between the Asante and the British or the fact that for the Asante involvement in the slave trade was a matter of self-preservation, as Lansiné Kaba explains:

> Ashanti and other kingdoms entered the slave trade not in order to exploit or victimize other Africans, but to survive the onslaught of European firearms. Furthermore, most of the individuals who participated directly belonged to the old or new elite of their society and acted primarily in their own interests.

The highly militarized nature of West African kingdoms such as Dahomey and Asante became necessary to survive the onslaught which Kaba mentions. Walter Rodney noted that "kings were just as likely to rob their own people as to attack their neighbours." Kingdoms that failed to protect their own citizens or engaged in the enslavement of their own citizens declined in the manner that Allada and Whydah did. Both of those kingdoms were eventually incorporated into Dahomey, which was one of the kingdoms which focused on protecting its citizens from the slave trade. Dahomey was able to withstand the onslaught, but the slave trade did take a toll on Dahomey's development. Dahomey suffered from famine and its population stagnated. In spite of this, Dahomey still managed to become one of the most powerful West African kingdoms during this period.

In all four examples cited by Gates we see that Africans were struggling against European domination in one form or another. We also see that some Africans wanted to turn to other business pursuits, but, ultimately, the Africans engaged in slave trading because it was the only form of business that the Europeans wished to pursue. Walter Rodney gives the following description:

Indirectly, via European testimony, the African rulers made it manifest that they regarded the slave trade as an imposition, but were prepared to pay that price for European goods. On this point, the Capuchins offered evidence which they elicited by questioning the African rulers on their attitude to the Atlantic slave trade. They found, as Barreira before them had done, that the African slavers recognized their profession for the evil it was, but contended that they indulged in man-stealing because the whites would purchase no other goods.

To reduce the slave trade to a partnership between Europeans and Africans ignores the centuries of wars and struggles against the European slave traders that Africans engaged in, and one certainly cannot say that there was equal blame on both sides. This is demonstrated by the fact that Europeans often ignored the requests of African rulers that did not wish to be drawn into the slave trade. Eric Williams wrote that "an African King of Senegal enacted a law that no slaves whatever should be marched through his territories." Williams also added that the law "remained a dead letter."

The slave trade became too powerful for any single African kingdom to resist. Apart from the examples of resistance that were previously noted, there was also the case of the Baga chief Tomba who attempted to organize resistance to the slave trade. He was captured and would later be killed after attempting a rebellion onboard one of the slave ships. The ruler of Benin sold female captives, but he was initially unwilling to sell male captives. This position later changed, however, and Benin began exporting male captives as well. Those who attempted to resist the slave trade were either defeated or forced into participating on the terms that the Europeans laid out.

That the Europeans dominated the slave trade, even at the expense of their African middle men, is demonstrated by a specific incident that lives on in the historical memory of the Anlo Ewe people of West Africa. This incident occurred at Atorkor. Chief Ndorkutsu had established trading relations with the Europeans for decades. Ndorkutsu had agents who would go inland, collect slaves, and bring them back to the shore where they would be transported by European and American ships. The Anlo Ewe never imagined that they could also be victims of the slave trade.

Ndorkutsu discovered, in 1856, that European slave traders had kidnapped some famous drummers from the community. These drummers included Ndorkutsu's grandson and grandfather. The slave traders had lured the drummers on the slave ship—some stories mention the use of food to entice the drummers. Once on the ship, the Europeans captured the drummers and then sailed away. Two of these drummers jumped overboard and drowned. The remaining drummers were sold in Cuba.

Another case of this trickery was of the African slave trader Daaga. Daaga was from the Popo nation in Dahomey. He was a slave trader who was tricked by the very slavers that he was selling slaves to. The Portuguese enticed him to come aboard their ship and Daaga was subsequently captured. The ship that he was on was intercepted by a British cruiser, and the cargo was taken to Trinidad. Daaga, who became a member of the West Indian Regiment, organized other Africans and led a mutiny in 1837. The mutiny was unsuccessful and Daaga was eventually captured and executed.

Gates writes that "slavery was a business, highly organized and lucrative for European buyers and African sellers alike." What Gates does not mention is that some of those wealthy African sellers were the mulattoes that were the offspring of the Europeans. These mulattoes straddled both European and African cultures, and they served as middle men for the Europeans traders. In some cases the mulattoes became rulers in Africa, and many of them were particularly noted for their ruthlessness. Therefore, to speak of the slave trade strictly as a business between European buyers and African sellers is to neglect the role of the mulatto middle men.

What the Europeans did with the slave trade was present it as a problem which was fundamentally African, so that they could make it appear as though they took it upon themselves to end this practice of slave trading. Eric Williams once observed that "British historians wrote almost as if Britain had introduced Negro slavery solely for the satisfaction of abolishing it." It is indeed strange how the people who profited the most from the Trans-Atlantic slave trade also boast about having done the most to end it too, but we find that even among a celebrated British abolitionist like William Wilberforce there was not a sincere concern for the African slaves. Wilberforce had initially affirmed that he only wanted to end the slave trade but not slavery itself. Moreover, the abolitionists generally favored a gradual approach to ending slavery.

This type of trickery and hypocrisy on the side of the British was not uncommon when dealing with Africans. There's one particular case in which the British served as the aggressor and then shifted the blame for the conflict on the Africans. This was the so-called Hut Tax War of 1898, in which a Temne chief named Bai Bureh is said to have revolted against the British when they imposed taxes on him. This certainly was not the case at all. In fact, by Bai Bureh's own account no one asked him to pay any taxes. He first became aware that there was a conflict when some of his own people were killed by Captain Sharpe. He also heard reports that Captain Sharpe was coming to kill him next.

Bai Bureh fought back in self-defense, but he was not the aggressor in this situation. He had been on peaceful terms with the British administration and even helped them in some of their wars, including a military expedition against the town of Tambi. Arthur Abraham sums up the situation between Bai and the British, writing:

> The sequence of events which led to Bai Bureh's involvement in the hostilities exposes unreasonableness and dishonor on the part of the British administration, and, contrary to official opinion, magnanimity on the part of the warrior. Bai Bureh was an innocent victim of the prejudices and designs of the frontiersmen of Pax Britannica.

If the Europeans went to Africa to civilize and pacify violent savages, they certainly failed in their mission and actually achieved the opposite. Many of the violent and bloody wars that we have seen in Africa during the post-colonial era have their roots in the increased warfare and aggression of slavery and colonialism in Africa. Despite all the claims that the Europeans made about civilizing Africa, they did more to disrupt those societies. Martin Delany perhaps summed up the situation best when, describing the impact of slavery on African people, he stated:

> But we have been, by our oppressors, despoiled of our purity, and corrupted in our native characteristics, so that we have inherited their vices, and but few of their virtues, leaving us in character, really a *broken people.*

Despite the image of Africa as a land of violent savages and cannibals, we find that there was a great level of humanity and hospitality in many African societies. In fact, part of the reason why the Europeans were able to so successfully conquer Africa the way that they did was because they were so well-received by the Africans. In most cases the Africans treated the Europeans like honored guests. They took the Europeans in, sheltered them, fed them, and in some cases they even gave the Europeans women to cohabitate with. In this regard, the Africans were naïve to the true intentions of many of the Europeans travelers, who would later enslave and oppress the very Africans that welcomed them. The Africa that the Europeans encountered was a land that was already civilized, but the land that Europeans left behind after colonization was a land wrecked with violence and instability.

Selected References

Abdallah Abdo Adou, "The Ethnic Factor in the National Politics of Djibouti," *The Oromo Commentary*, Vol II. No. 1, 1992

Adam Hochschild, *King Leopold's Ghost*, (New York: Mariner Books, 1998).

Ana Lucia Araujo, "Dahomey, Portugal and Bahia: King Adandozan and the Atlantic Slave Trade," *A Journal of Slave and Post-Slave Studies*, 33:1, 1-19

Anne Bailey, *African Voices of the Atlantic Slave Trade*, (Beacon Press, 2006).

Arthur Abraham, "Bai Bureh, The British, and the Hut Tax War," *The International Journal of African Historical Studies*, Vol. 7, no. 1 (1974): pp. 99-106

Augustus A. Adeyinka, "King Gezo of Dahomey, 1818-1858: A Reassessment of a West African Monarch in the Nineteenth Century," *African Studies Review*, Vol. 17, No. 3 (Dec., 1974), pp. 541-548

Boniface I. Obichere, "The Social Character of Slavery in Asante and Dahomey," *Ufahamu: A Journal of African Studies*, 12 (3), 1983.

Chancellor Williams, *The Destruction of Black Civilization*, (Chicago: Third World Press, 1987).

Collin A. Palmer, *Eric Williams and the Making of the Modern Caribbean*, (The University of North Carolina Press, 2008).

Cornelius Vijn, *Cetshawayo's Dutchman: Being the Private Journal of a White Trader in Zululand During the British Invasion*, (London: 1880).

David Lopes, "The Destruction of the Kingdom of Kongo," *Civil Rights Journal*, volume 6, no. 1, 2002 pp. 31-39

Edward Alexander Powell, *The Last Frontier: The White Man's War for Civilization in Africa*, 1916.

E.G. Ravenstein, *The Strange Adventures of Andrew Battell of Leigh in Angola and the Adjoining Regions*

Eric Williams, *History of the People of Trinidad and Tobago*, 1962.

Emil Torday, *On the Trail of the Bushongo*, 1925.

Frank Snowden, "Greeks and Ethiopians," *Greeks and Barbarians*, J.E. Coleman and C.A. Walz (ed.), 1997

George McCall Theal, *"Records of South-Eastern Africa: collected in various libraries and archive departments in Europe, Volume 3,"* (Printed for the Government of the Cape Colony, 1899).

Henry Louis Gates, "Ending the Slavery Blame-Game," *New York Times*, April 22, 2010

James Frederick Cunningham, *Uganda and Its People*, 1905.

Joseph Casely Hayford, *Gold Coast Native Institutions: With Thoughts Upon a Healthy Imperial Policy for the Gold Coast and Ashanti*, (London: Sweet and Maxwell, Limited, 1903).

John Bird, *The Annals of Natal: 1495 to 1845*, Volume 1, (P. Davis & Sons, 1888).

John K. Thornton, "Elite Women in the Kingdom of Kongo:

Historical Perspectives on Women's Political Power," *The Journal of African History*, Vol. 47, No. 3 (2006), pp. 437-460

___"Legitimacy and Political Power: Queen Njinga, 1624-1663", *The Journal of Africa History*, Vol. 32, No. 1 (1991), pp.25-40

Julius Nyerere, *"Ujamaa": The Basis of African Socialism*, 1962.

Lansiné Kaba, "The Atlantic Slave Trade Was Not a 'Black-on-Black Holocaust'", *African Studies Review*, Vol. 44, No. 1 (Apr., 2001), pp. 1-20

Martin Delany, *Official Report of the Niger Valley Exploring Party*, 1861.

___*The Condition, Elevation, Emigration, and Destiny of the Colored People of the United States*

Mary Kingsley, *Travels in West Africa*, 1897.

___West African Studies (London: The Macmillan Company, 1899).

Mitch Keller, "The Scandal at the Zoo," *New York Times*, August 6, 2006.

Olaudah Equiano, *The Interesting Narrative of the Life of Olaudah Equiano*, 1789.

Paul Magnarella, "Explaining Rwanda's 1994 Genocide" *Human Rights & Human Welfare*, Volume 2:1, 2002.

Rt. Rev. MacBaker Ochola II, "Spirit of Reconciliation: A Case Study of Mato Oput"

Robin Law, "Human Sacrifice in Pre-Colonial West Africa," *African Affairs*, Vol. 84, No. 334 (1985), pp. 53-87

Samuel Johnson, *The History of the Yorubas*. (London: Routledge and Kegan Paul, 1921).

Stephanie Smallwood, *Saltwater Slavery: A Middle Passage from Africa to American Diaspora*, (Harvard University Press, 2008).

Thomas Collelo (editor), *Angola: A Country Study*, Washington: GPO for the Library of Congress, 1991.

Walter Rodney, *A History of the Upper Guinea Coast, 1545 to 1800*, (Oxford University Press, 1970).

___*How Europe Underdeveloped Africa*, (Bogle-L'Ouverture Publications, 1972).

___*The Groundings with My Brothers*, (Frontline Distribution International, 1969).

W.E.B. Du Bois, *Dusk of Dawn: An Essay Toward An Autobiography of a Race Concept*, (Harcourt, Brace & World, Inc., 1940).

___*The Negro*, (New York: Holt, 1915).

___*The Suppression of the African Slave-Trade To the United States of America 1638-1870*, (Longmans & Co., 1896).

Wilfrid D. Hambly, *The Ovimbundu of Angola*

2

THE STRENGTHS AND WEAKNESSES OF THE NATION OF ISLAM

"Malcolm X and Elijah Muhammad's message made a whole lot of people feel whole again, human being again. Some of them came out and found a new meaning to their manhood and their womanhood."
-John Henrik Clarke

"We, the Black people in America, do not think for self first. Failing to think for self first is the greatest mistake we the poor Black people who are up from servitude slavery of the fathers can make."
-Elijah Muhammad

"Many blacks who converted took to the Nation's teachings—its admonitions to self-love and racial solidarity; its belief in productivity and entrepreneurship. Using the twin motivators of myth and pride, Elijah Muhammad built the Nation into one of the largest black economic and religious organizations America had seen. [...] Its women looked like angels in their veils, crisp jackets and ankle-length skirts; its men cut no-nonsense yet gallant figures in their smart dark suits and trademark bow ties."
-Steven Barboza

Elijah Muhammad took over the leadership of the Nation of Islam in 1934 following the sudden disappearance of Wallace Fard Muhammad, the Nation of Islam's founder. There is a lot of controversy surrounding the background of Fard. There is no information concerning where and when he was born. Some have argued that Wallace Fard Muhammad was just one of the many aliases that he used. Even his sudden disappearance remains a mystery. What is most definitely clear is that Fard founded the Nation of Islam in the 1930s and among his converts was Elijah Poole, later named Elijah Muhammad. It was under Elijah

Muhammad's leadership that the Nation of Islam became a nationally recognized movement.

The Nation of Islam as an organization can best be understood when one looks at the time period around when the organization was founded. The Nation of Islam was one of a number of organizations to emerge in the wake of Marcus Garvey's deportation from the United States. Garvey's deportation created a leadership void that was replaced by a number of religious organizations that contained elements of Garvey's movement. The Nation of Islam was one such movement, but it was by no means the only one or even the first one to emerge.

The Nation of Islam was one of the most notable of these organizations and the similarities with the Garvey movement are obvious. Like the Universal Negro Improvement Association (UNIA), the Nation of Islam heavily emphasized racial pride and economic self-reliance as critical elements to the liberation of black people. The organizational structures of both organizations shared certain similarities as well, as Theodore G. Vincent explains: "The Nation of Islam included many features which were present in the UNIA. The Muslim defense corps, the Fruit of Islam, is analogous to the UNIA's African Legions and police force."

The similarities between the ideologies of the two movements naturally drew some former Garveyites to Elijah Muhammad's movement. The family of Malcolm X is an example of this. Both of Malcolm's parents were Garveyites and that influence stayed with Malcolm's siblings. His brother Wilfred declared that the Nation of Islam was attractive to him and his siblings because they had already "been indoctrinated with the Marcus Garvey's philosophy" and they did not have to be convinced to be black and proud. Some sources state that Elijah Muhammad himself was a member of the UNIA. Some claim that he was a member of the Chicago division of the UNIA, while others remember him as a member of the Detroit branch. Elijah Muhammad also held Garvey (and Noble Drew Ali of the Moorish American Science Temple) in high-esteem, stating:

> I have always had a very high opinion of both the late Noble Drew Ali and Marcus Garvey and admired their courage in helping our people (the so-called Negroes) and appreciated their work. Both of these men were fine Muslims. The followers of Noble Drew Ali and Marcus Garvey should now follow me and cooperate with us in our work because we are only trying to finish up what those before us started.

This statement from Elijah Muhammad is curious for two reasons. The first of which is the reference to Garvey as being a fine Muslim, when Garvey was in fact not a Muslim. This leaves us to wonder whether Elijah Muhammad actually believed that Garvey was a Muslim or if Elijah Muhammad merely referred to Garvey as a Muslim to demonstrate the similarities between the ideological thought of the Nation of Islam and Garvey. The second reason that this statement is an interesting one is that Elijah Muhammad casts himself as the successor of both men and suggests that their followers should now follow him. In fact, historian Tony Martin explains that Elijah Muhammad "did some of his early proselytizing in Chicago in 1933 in a UNIA Liberty Hall." Noble Drew Ali had engaged in a similar tactic in trying to draw support from former Garveyites by claiming that he was continuing the work of Garvey. Drew Ali was so successful at this that many Garveyites had requested that American authorities allow Garvey to return to the United States so that he could challenge the Moorish American Science Temple. By the time Elijah Muhammad took control of the Nation of Islam, Garvey was exiled from the United States and Noble Drew Ali was dead, leaving Elijah Muhammad free to attract the former followers of both men.

The Moorish American Science Temple shared many similarities with the ideology of the Nation of Islam. The most apparent similarity is that both organizations were an ideological blend of Black Nationalism and Islam. Both organizations also held the view that black people needed a separate nation of their own, and they both believed that the separate and independent nation in question was to be carved out in the United States. Like the Nation of Islam, Drew Ali also told his followers that they

60

were Asiatics rather than "Negroes" and that Islam was the religion that belonged to them.

Internal disputes arose within the Moorish American Science Temple and it resulted in Drew Ali's main rival being stabbed and shot to death. Drew Ali, who was jailed in relation to that murder, himself later died under mysterious circumstances. The Nation of Islam emerged in the wake of the Moorish American Science Temple's collapse and there was a direct link between the two organizations, as many Moors made up some of the earliest converts to the Nation of Islam. The Nation of Islam's founder, Wallace Fard Muhammad, has sometimes been identified as a former follower of the Moorish American Science Temple, although this has been denied by the Nation of Islam.

Another religious movement that is comparable to the Nation of Islam was the movement led by Father Divine, who declared himself to be God. Father Divine was able to attract many former Garveyites through his emphasis on economic self-reliance. Father Divine established a successful communal movement, which managed to feed and provide housing for thousands of people. This is especially significant given that Father Divine's Peace Mission operated in the 1930s, in the midst of the Great Depression. Father Divine owned restaurants, laundries, and communal farms that employed his followers.

Father Divine's organization was also one of contradictions. Father Divine had preached celibacy and even segregated the sexes in his communal living quarters. Even husbands and wives were made to live separately. Yet Father Divine had married, twice. Although Father Divine had taught his followers never to concern themselves with money, he was himself a very wealthy man. He flaunted this wealth by wearing expensive suits, living in large estates, and driving expensive cars.

The similarity between Father Divine's organization and the Nation of Islam is very apparent. These were two organizations that practiced economic self-reliance and provided food, employment, shelter, and other material benefits to their followers.

These were both organizations that were primarily concerned with religious matters, but were both able to garner a large following due to these same material benefits. The religious views of both organizations also draw similarities concerning the concept of God. Father Divine proclaimed himself to be God, not unlike how Elijah Muhammad had proclaimed that Fard Muhammad was God. In both organizations God was embodied in the person of both organizations' founders.

Father Divine's movement also differed from the Nation of Islam and the UNIA in key ways. The most notable of which was that Father Divine did not preach a Black Nationalist movement. He actually had a large number of white followers, although the organization was primarily comprised of black people. Father Divine publicly declared that he did not distinguish on the basis of race, which made many former Garveyites reluctant to join. Father Divine had even married a white woman. And whereas the Nation of Islam stressed the fact that God was a black man as opposed to the white image of God that black people had been indoctrinated with, Father Divine did not place any importance on the fact that he, a black man, was God. Father Divine never attempted to undo the inferiority complex in black people as the Nation of Islam had done.

Like the Nation of Islam, Father Divine's movement attracted people from the ghettos that had engaged in a number of destructive and immoral behaviors. Father Divine's followers were made to cease engaging in crime, gambling, prostitution, alcoholism, and drug addiction. These were all things that the Nation of Islam had prohibited their followers from engaging in, as well. Where the two organizations differed was that Father Divine taught his followers that they were responsible for their own misfortunes and that belief in Father Divine would redeem and protect them. The Nation of Islam, on the other hand, took the position that centuries of white oppression was responsible for the plight and destructive behaviors of impoverished black people.

Yet another key difference was found in religion. Both organizations were obviously rooted in the idea of the divinity of their leaders, with Father Divine literally preaching that he was God and Elijah Muhammad preaching that he was Allah's messenger. Elijah Muhammad had emphasized that his ascension as the leader of the Nation of Islam was fulfillment of prophecy and that God would soon return to liberate black people from white oppression. Father Divine, on the other hand, proclaimed that he had already brought a new world into existence and that all his people needed to do to be saved was to follow him. Where the Nation of Islam preached of an impending destruction of white America for its wicked deeds committed against black people, Father Divine preached a doctrine of redemption.

There were a number of factors that set apart the Nation of Islam from the other two religious organizations. Noble Drew Ali concerned himself with instilling pride and a new sense of identity in black people, as well as the creation of an independent black nation, but unlike the UNIA, the Moorish Science Temple did not emphasize the building of a strong economic base. The Nation of Islam did, however. Father Divine's Peace Mission, on the other hand, fed, sheltered, and employed his followers. His movement was one that was largely self-reliant, but this was not a Black Nationalist organization like the UNIA was. Father Divine happened to attract a large black following, but his movement was not specifically targeted towards addressing issues such as racial discrimination or the inferiority complex of black people. This is not to say that Father Divine completely distanced himself from issues such as racial discrimination and lynching, but these issues were not at the forefront of his movement's goals. Unlike the Peace Mission, the Nation of Islam took up the ideology of "race first" that Garvey had promoted.

Although the Nation of Islam was primarily a religious organization like the Moorish American Science Temple and the Peace Mission, it was also a more politically oriented movement as well. The Nation of Islam did not encourage its members to become actively engaged in the political process, but this did not stop the organization from taking political positions. They were vocally critical of America's political process, critical of civil rights leaders, and some of their members had even been jailed for refusing to fight in America's various wars. The rhetoric of the Nation of Islam also had an impact on the civil rights movement. Malcolm explained that although the Nation of Islam did not do much beyond reforming its members, the rhetoric used by the movement was such that they "made the whole civil-rights movement become more militant, and more acceptable to the white power structure." Malcolm also explained that the Nation of Islam may have "forced many of the civil-rights leaders to be even more militant than they intended." So although the Nation of Islam was not a very politically action oriented organization, it did leave a lasting impact on the mainstream civil rights struggle. By comparison the Peace Mission and Moorish Science Temple were strictly religious movements that had little lasting impact on the political struggle of black people.

What we have seen here is that the Nation of Islam was not the first organization of its type. Rather it was one of many of the religious organizations that rose following the decline of Garvey's movement. Of the three religious movements that were discussed, the Nation of Islam was the one that had the most in common with the UNIA in that it was both an organization that sought to restore the self-esteem of black people and create a self-reliant economic base. Of the three organizations, it was also the one that had the greatest political impact in the struggle for black liberation. It was the one that provided the greatest challenge to the white supremacist structure of the United States. The Nation of Islam was also able to achieve the greatest lasting impact of these three religious organizations due, in large part, to spokespersons such as Malcolm X, Muhammad Ali, and Louis Farrakhan that were able to acquire a following that went beyond the Nation of Islam itself.

One of the greatest strengths of the Nation of Islam was its ability to reform and reshape the consciousness of its followers. It took people from the ghettos that were engaging in a number of self-defeating behaviors and turned them towards productive behaviors. The organization also reformed many criminals. C.E. Lincoln explains: "The regeneration of criminals and other fallen persons is a prime concern of the Black Muslims, and they have an enviable record of success." After his break with the Nation of Islam, Malcolm still found this program of social reform to be one of the greatest strengths of the movement. Although he expressed regret over what the Nation of Islam became and his role in developing what he came to view as a criminal organization, Malcolm did not take away the fact that it was an organization that had immense spiritual power and the ability to reform its followers:

> It was not a criminal organization at the outset. It was an organization that had the power, the spiritual power, to reform the criminal. And this is what you have to understand. As long as that strong spiritual power was in the movement, it gave the moral strength to the believer that would enable him to rise above all his negative tendencies. I know, because I went into the movement with more negative tendencies than anybody in the movement [...] And by this spiritual force, giving one the faith that enabled one to exercise some moral discipline, it became an organization that was to be respected as well as feared.

Under the leadership of Elijah Muhammad, the Nation of Islam was an organization that was able to change the consciousness of its members. It rehabilitated drug addicts, criminals, prostitutes, and other people that society had ignored. The teachings of Elijah Muhammad gave these people a new sense of self-worth. A woman who worked as a prostitute prior to joining the Nation of Islam explained her experience in the movement as follows:

> Respect and love showed to Black women by the members of NOI played a great part in making me become Muslim. Some of them knew my past but it did not matter. I had never seen and experienced an acceptance as a sister and a person with such sincerity and warm environment as shown by brothers and sisters in the Nation.

Malcolm X was the most famous example of the Nation of Islam's ability to change the mentality and consciousness of its followers. This was a man who prior to becoming a Muslim had been a criminal and a drug addict. He was arrested and jailed for burglary and in prison his temperament was such that he was given the nickname "Satan." It was during his time in prison that Malcolm was first exposed to the Nation of Islam. In the teachings of Elijah Muhammad, Malcolm found a belief system that gave him a sense of identity and a level of confidence in himself that made him rise above his criminal mentality. In his autobiography Malcolm explained the influence that Elijah Muhammad's teachings had on him as follows: "When I was a foul, vicious convict, so evil that other convicts had called me Satan, this man had rescued me. He was the man who had trained me, who had treated me as if I were his own flesh and blood. He was the man who had given me wings—to go places, to do things I otherwise never would have dreamed of."

We can also look at Muhammad Ali as an example. Elijah Muhammad's message took the brash and boastful Cassius Clay and made him into the internationally respected Muhammad Ali. Ali was a great boxer without the influence of the Nation of Islam, but it was the Nation of Islam that gave Ali the conviction and courage to take the moral stance that he did when he refused to go to Vietnam, choosing instead to face jail time. The Nation of Islam turned Ali into an uncompromising voice against injustice.

This was a champion that stood up against racism and the mistreatment of black people, and the contrast between Ali and other contemporary boxers was clear. Whereas Ali changed his slave name, other boxers not only wore their slave names, but they also refused to acknowledge Ali's new name. Floyd Patterson, Ernie Terrell, and Joe Frazier all continued to call Ali by his birth name; Cassius Clay. Ali responded by labeling all three men as Uncle Toms. Floyd Patterson, who was a Catholic, went so far to declare that he wanted to defeat Ali to prevent the championship from being held by a Muslim. Malcolm commented on this by describing Patterson as a "brainwashed black Christian" who was ready to do battle for the white man. Patterson also tried to move into a white neighborhood, but later ended up moving out due to the terrible way in which his white neighbors treated him. Ali, on the other hand, rejected integration, Christianity, and his slave name. Ali was also more vocal in addressing racial and social issues than other contemporary boxers were.

Muhammad Ali was a world famous boxer that had been vocal on issues that were afflicting the black community, but the battle that really turned him into a political figure was fought outside the ring. Ali was drafted to go to Vietnam, but he refused on the grounds of his religious beliefs. For this Ali was stripped of the heavyweight championship and his boxing license was revoked. This was a sacrifice that Ali was willing to make and in doing so Ali was able to both express the Nation of Islam's policy concerning warfare, as well as win favor with anti-war activists. Martin Luther King, who had been critical of Ali's religious beliefs, came to respect Ali's stance on the war. Both men united on their criticisms of what they saw as an unjust war. The Vietnam War proved to be a very unpopular war for a number of reasons. The war had suffered from mission creep, in which the ultimate objectives of the war were both unclear and frequently changing. Also adding to the war's unpopularity was the institution of a draft.

The Nation of Islam had long since taken the position that it was unjust for America to draft black people to fight in America's wars. This position was both a religious one and political one. Religiously, the Nation of Islam objected to wars which took the lives of other humans. Politically, the Nation of Islam recognized that America was oppressing and brutalizing the very black people that they were sending to war. Muhammad Ali's statement, "I don't have no personal quarrel with those Viet Congs" was a direct reflection of the Nation of Islam's position that their enemies were not people in a foreign land, their enemies were the white men that had enslaved and oppressed them within the United States. Muhammad Ali was not the only member of the Nation of Islam to go to jail for refusing to go to war. Elijah Muhammad spent several years in prison for sedition because he had told his followers not to register for the draft during World War II. We cannot say for certain what Ali's position on the Vietnam War would have been had he not joined the Nation of Islam, but Ali's views on the war and his decision to go to jail rather than take part in what he considered to be an unjust war was definitely due to the influence of the Nation of Islam's teachings.

Elijah Muhammad taught his followers to quit smoking—although the Nation of Islam banned members from smoking, Malcolm observed that when he went to Mecca, Arab Muslims smoked almost constantly. This not only urged the Muslims to quit a dangerous habit, but they also ceased spending money on something destructive and spent it on more constructive pursuits such as building and owning their own businesses. The Nation of Islam did not only ban drugs, but it excelled in cleaning up drug addicts. Their program worked so well that some social agencies had actually asked Muslim representatives for clinical suggestions in dealing with drug addicts.

The drug treatment program of the Nation of Islam was successful because the Muslims worked around-the-clock shifts to tend to the addict as the addict went through the whole ordeal. As the addict was enduring withdrawals, the Muslim would be by their side the whole time giving him words of advice and encouragement. Afterwards, the Muslim stayed with the addict and helped to nurse them back to health. When the addict had fully recovered, the ex-addict usually joined the Nation of Islam and set about continuing the work of curing other addicts of their addictions, thus creating a cycle. Muslim sisters were also involved in this process. They would rehabilitate dope addicted women who prostituted themselves for money.

Elijah Muhammad also turned his followers away from unhealthy foods, particularly pork. Elijah Muhammad published *How to Eat to Live*, which gave Muslims instructions about how to maintain a proper and healthy diet. One of the dietary practices that Elijah Muhammad taught his followers was to eat only once a day because that way they would not overeat. He told his readers: "Take time and prepare your own foods. Do not kill yourselves by running to the store buying processed foods to eat, and never buy those ready made biscuits." Elijah Muhammad also points out that: "The European white race, blessed with the privilege of eating the best food the earth provides, has taught us to eat the worst (divinely prohibited) food."

Elijah Muhammad was making his followers conscious about their diet which was a much needed lesson given that during slavery black people survived mainly on the scraps that were given to them by their slave masters. The terrible diet that was fed to slaves is something that Elijah Muhammad mentioned frequently in *How to Eat to Live*. There was also an economic function to this as well because the Nation of Islam had farmland, groceries, and restaurants that catered to the appetites of Muslims. In this regard, Elijah Muhammad not only told his followers to eat better, but the Nation of Islam provided the means that allowed them to eat better while also putting their money back to their own community.

The Nation of Islam was an organization that sought to eliminate all of the unhealthy, unproductive, and destructive habits of its members. An elder member of the organization named Raymond explained:

> It [the Nation of Islam] made me realize I wasn't no Negro, it made me realize this was a stigma....the Honorable Elijah Muhammad made us know that we were the original people of the earth, which when you learn that, you really feel proud and don't want to be nobody but who you are... I was a reefer smoker, I drank liquor, I gambled, I did all them things, I chased women and he [Elijah Muhammad] stopped me from doing all of that...

Aside from being an organization that stressed moral reform, the Nation of Islam also preached and practiced self-reliance. They owned bakeries, a barber shop, grocery stores, restaurants, retail stores, and farmland. They also had their own schools and a national newspaper. Therefore, we see within the program of the Nation of Islam that it not only rehabilitated its members, but it produced black owned businesses and encouraged economic self-reliance and self-sufficiency. This proved to be beneficial to the black community at large, as even non-Muslims were employed by

69

the businesses that were owned by the Nation of Islam. A member of the Nation of Islam named Hakeem attested to the fact that the Nation of Islam hired people that were not part of the movement:

> When the Nation bought that bank, the Messenger had put out the word that this wasn't just for Muslims and even when the [Muhammad Speaks] Press hired, we hired just as many non-Muslims as we did Muslims and even when the bank opened he [Elijah Muhammad] said if a person had a job if they applied for a loan let them have the loan you know—and that just wasn't to the Muslims, that was to the community.

Elijah Muhammad introduced a Twelve Point Program in which he outlined his economic philosophy. Among some of the points in this plan was for black people to stop forcing themselves where they were not wanted and to pool their resources together to build up their own communities. Included in this Twelve Point Program were urges to shun racial integration and demands for black people to protect their women. Elijah Muhammad also laid out a Three Year Economic program. This program urged black people to limit their spending on clothes and shoes. The money that black people saved was then encouraged to be used to purchase land to grow vegetables and raise cattle. Along with farmland, Elijah Muhammad also encouraged buying timberland in order to use the timber for building houses.

Some critics of the Nation of Islam have argued that Elijah Muhammad's economic policies were primarily concerned with enriching the organization's leader. Indeed, one of the growing criticisms of Elijah Muhammad within the Nation of Islam was the fact that he had amassed such a large fortune for himself and his family. Some Muslims began to feel like the wealth within the Nation of Islam was too unequally distributed. Despite this, Elijah Muhammad's followers did reap many benefits from their association with the Nation of Islam. They had their own schools, businesses, and other institutions that were designed to make them more independent from white people—this is especially significant given the struggles that black people endured for things such as employment and proper education. Muslims also very obviously benefited from Elijah Muhammad's teachings on healthy living. Raymond responded to these criticisms of Elijah Muhammad by explaining: "He [Elijah Muhammad] stopped making me smoke reefer, stop me from smoking cigarettes, stop me from drinking liquor and everything else. Now who benefitted from that, he or me?"

Members of the Nation of Islam also benefited from the movement in financial ways as well. Nafeesa Haniyah Muhammad interviewed a former member of the Nation of Islam named Joseph, who joined the movement in 1970. Joseph was attracted to the Nation of Islam because of its teachings on self-sufficiency. Joseph explained that listening to the teachings of Elijah Muhammad was "one of the first times that I've ever heard uh encouraging instructions to stand up and do something for yourself, for yourself and to be self reliant and determine your own destiny and that help me to understand what a man was and I had the faith." He also credited Elijah Muhammad with making him a more disciplined man, a better husband and father, and an all-round better human being.

Despite some of the positive aspects of the Nation of Islam's economic program, there were certain limitations to just how much economic success was achieved by the movement. Aubrey Barnette was a former member of the Nation of Islam, but he split with the organization and wrote an article titled "The Black Muslims Are a Fraud." One of the things that most disillusioned him with the movement was what he called "the economic myth." Barnette went into the movement as a college graduate with a degree in business administration. He was disappointed to see that the businesses that the Nation of Islam were boasting about consisted of only a grocery store, a barbershop, a restaurant, and a dress factory. He explained: "Now I was greatly disillusioned when I saw these things [...] this was the extent of the great Muslim empire that they had been speaking about."

Malcolm X also pointed to the financial difficulties that the movement went through. Malcolm explained that most of the businesses that the Nation of Islam owned "operated in the red." Many of these businesses also folded and Malcolm stated that Elijah Muhammad had to subsidize many of the businesses that the Nation of Islam operated in Chicago. So there certainly were financial difficulties experienced within the movement and the financial struggles of many of the members combined with the wealth that Elijah Muhammad's family had amassed contributed to tensions and dissatisfaction during the latter years of Elijah Muhammad's leadership.

The transformative element of the Nation of Islam lay in the psychologically uplifting aspects of the teachings of Elijah Muhammad. Elijah Muhammad's teachings addressed the reality that his followers were a religious people that came from a Christian background, yet he understood that within this same Christianity was a doctrine that reinforced the low self-esteem of African Americans. He stated:

> One of the first and most important truths that must be established in this day is our identity. This is what our God, Whose Proper Name is Allah, is guiding me to point out to you, my people, who are members of the Lost and Found Nation in North America. You, my people, who have been robbed of your complete identity for over 400 years. Is it not time for you to know who you are after 400 years of submission to the white slave-masters of America and their false religion of Christianity?

The abolitionist Martin Delany once observed "that there are no people more religious in this Country, than the colored people, and none so poor and miserable as they." Martin Delany also wrote of encountering an African who told him: "Of what use is the white man's religion and 'book knowledge' to me, since it does not give me the knowledge and wisdom nor the wealth and power of the white man, as all these things belong only to him? Our young men and women learn their book, and talk on paper (write), and talk to God like white man (worship), but God no hear 'em like He hear white man! Dis religion no use to black man." This particular

African recognized that although his people took on the white man's religion and the white man's reading and writing, it was truly of no use for the black man because he was still not as rich as the white man nor were his people as powerful or smart as the white man. This is because merely practicing the European religion and learning European writing is not enough for African people to progress. Christianity itself did not advance the Europeans; it was the means by which they used Christianity as a tool (or better yet, a weapon) to advance their interests that caused them to progress. It is within this context that we can come to understand how Elijah Muhammad used Islam as a tool for social change.

In his work *The Souls of Black Folk*, W.E.B. Du Bois explained how Christianity was used to quell the rebellious nature of the slaves:

> In spite, however, of such success as that of the fierce Maroons, the Danish blacks, and others, the spirit of revolt gradually died away under the untiring energy and superior strength of the slave masters. By the middle of the eighteenth century the black slave had sunk, with hushed murmurs, to his place at the bottom of a new economic system, and was unconsciously ripe for a new philosophy of life. Nothing suited his condition then better than the doctrines of passive submission embodied in the newly learned Christianity. Slave masters early realized this, and cheerfully aided religious propaganda within certain bounds.

This was the type of condition that Elijah Muhammad contended with. In doing so, Elijah Muhammad formulated his own version of Islam that suited both the material and psychological needs of his followers. Although Elijah Muhammad claimed that all of his teachings were given to him by Fard Muhammad, it appears that Elijah Muhammad had in fact added some ideas of his own to Fard's teachings. When Elijah Muhammad took control of the

73

Nation of Islam, he began preaching that Fard Muhammad was God incarnated as a man. Fard himself had never claimed to be Allah.

According to the teachings of the Nation of Islam, Wallace Fard Muhammad gave Elijah Muhammad knowledge of the true history of black people. Fard Muhammad then vanished, leaving Elijah Muhammad to preach Fard's message to black people throughout the United States. For this reason Elijah Muhammad taught his followers that he was the messenger of God. This was one of the major controversies with Elijah Muhammad's teachings and a great example of the psychological impact that Elijah Muhammad's teachings had. Elijah Muhammad had declared that God was not only a man, but a black man. Psychologically this made sense given that Christianity affirmed white supremacy in the minds of black people. This is why when speaking about the Nation of Islam, Malcolm explained: "We don't separate our religion from our color nor do we separate our color from our religion [...] the white man never has separated Christianity from white, nor has he separated white from Christianity." Malcolm went on to explain that his parents sang songs such as "Wash Me White As Snow." To give yet another example of this, in his "Ballot or the Bullet" speech, given after Malcolm X left the Nation of Islam but before he embraced orthodox Islam, Malcolm explained that Billy Graham preached White Nationalism because everyone in Graham's church was depicted as white, including Jesus and Mary. Malcolm recognized that Christianity was used to fill black people with the desire to be white, therefore Malcolm described Elijah Muhammad's teachings as being "designed to undo the type of brainwashing that we have had to undergo for four hundred years at the hands of the white man in order to bring us down to the level that we're on today."

Eurocentric Christianity was dominated by imagery of white angels, white saints, and even a white Jesus, which according to the doctrine of Christianity was God incarnated as a man. In other words, the people that Elijah Muhammad was dealing with had already been taught that God was a white man, which was damaging to their own self-image. It may have been controversial, but in preaching that God was a black man Elijah Muhammad was undoing a major aspect of Eurocentric Christianity's teachings. He was not alone in this process either. Other Black Nationalists had challenged the notion of a white Jesus, without necessarily rejecting Christianity altogether. For example, Reverend Albert Cleage and James R. Lawson had promoted images of a black Jesus. Like Elijah Muhammad, they recognized the importance of religious imagery in the self-esteem of a people.

More controversial than his claim that God was a black man was that Elijah Muhammad taught his followers that the devil that is spoken of in the Bible was actually the white race. According to the teachings of the Nation of Islam, whites were created by a mad scientist named Yacub. As a youngster Yacub had decided that one day he would create a new race of people that would rule over black people. According to Elijah Muhammad's teachings it was predetermined that Yacub would create this new race of man.

At the age of sixteen, Yacub began preaching all over Arabia and created confusion. The confusion was so great that Yacub's followers were jailed and eventually Yacub himself was jailed by the king. Realizing that it was prophecy that Yacub had to create a new race, the king knew there was nothing that he could do to stop Yacub so he had Yacub exiled on an island in the Aegean Sea. Yacub took 59,999 of his followers to that island where he began his experiment to create a new race of people.

According to the Nation of Islam, Jacob in the Bible was Yacub. The story of Jacob wrestling with an angel is presented by the Nation of Islam as being a symbolic representation of Yacub wrestling with the government of his day. Just as Jacob was able to overcome the angel until the angel cheated by throwing Jacob's hip out of place, so too did Yacub overcome the government that he fought with and although Yacub was exiled, the king ended up giving Yacub everything that he needed for his experiment. This story also presents a parallel between Yacub's struggle with the government of his time and Elijah Muhammad's own demands that the American government give the Nation of Islam everything that they need to create a separate state.

Now in exile and having been given the necessary supplies by the king of Arabia, Yacub began conducting his experiment of grafting away the "black germ" until he created a new white race. The part in the Bible where God declares "let us make man" is interpreted by the Nation of Islam to be not God, but Yacub talking to his followers about creating a new race of men that would rule the world for about 6,000 years. Yacub, who lived for 150 years, died before this process was completed, but he left behind instructions for his followers. After a few centuries of experimentation, the black germ had been finally grafted into a white one.

Although Yacub died, he left whites with a science called "tricknology" which they would use to divide and conquer black people through spreading false rumors about them to each other. Once black people began fighting and killing each other based on those lies, the white man would then act as the mediator. The Nation of Islam's teachings state that white people went to Arabia where they began to spread lies and within six months they had created chaos. The king recognized that the people creating confusion in Arabia were Yacub's people. The king decided to round up all of the white people and force them out of Arabia into Europe.

The story of Adam being put out of the Garden of Eden for disobeying God is presented by the Nation of Islam as an allegory for what happened to white people at the hands of the Arabian king. They were prevented from returning to the east by an angel with a flaming sword. White people moved into the caves of Europe, where the Nation of Islam teaches that they became beasts that walked around on all fours. They had forgotten to walk upright and eventually grew tails. Elijah Muhammad also explained that during this time the only other beast in Europe that befriended whites were dogs.

According to the Nation of Islam's teachings Moses did not go to Egypt. He actually went to Europe where he civilized white people. He taught white people a number of things, which included the same tricknology that Yacub had originally created. Moses also informed white people that a messiah would come to destroy them. According to the Nation of Islam, this was why the Jews had Jesus crucified. They feared that he was the messiah that Moses warned them about.

The rule of white people was to last 6,000 years until God returned in the person of Wallace Fard Muhammad to teach Elijah Muhammad the true history of the black man. The goal of Elijah Muhammad was to use these teachings to build up an independent nation that was to separate from whites so that when God returned, he could finally liberate black people from the wicked rule of whites. This is a summary of what Elijah Muhammad taught his followers concerning the history of black people and their oppression at the hands of whites. The story does utilize some of the Bible's narratives, but it is very obviously a mythology that is wholly unique to the Nation of Islam. Although the Nation of Islam considered the Bible and the Quran to be holy books, they also felt that the books had been written in a symbolic language that was not meant to be taken entirely literally. For the Nation of Islam, the Bible stories served as allegories for what they considered to be real history.

Not taken literally, however, we can see why Elijah Muhammad's narrative was so appealing to his followers. Traditional narratives about the enslavement of black people presented black people as being savages and cannibals in the jungles of Africa. Elijah Muhammad told black people that they descended from kings and queens. He told his followers that they were once in control of great civilizations. In this respect, he gave his followers a sense of history and identity which allowed them to have pride in themselves. Elijah Muhammad explained that instilling pride in his followers was precisely the goal of his religious teachings: "The so-called American Negro have to be completely re-educated and Islam gives him that qualification that he can feel proud and does not feel ashamed to be called a black man."

The type of Islam that the Nation of Islam was preaching obviously differed from traditional Islam, but for what Elijah Muhammad intended to do, his teachings were effective. To begin with, it provided a much needed alternative to the mostly Eurocentric Christian ideas that black people were being indoctrinated with. The religion of Islam also brought with it a sense of reclaiming that which was taken from black people. Black people were forced to become Christians at the expense of losing whatever religions they had previously practiced. In this regard, converting to Islam was seen as returning to what Elijah Muhammad had explained was the true religion of the black man.

There is a bit of truth in this claim, as some of the enslaved Africans that came to America were Muslims. Two examples of this were Omar ibn Said and Abdul Rahman Ibrahima Sori. Omar ibn Said was born in Futa Toro where he grew up and eventually became an Islamic scholar. Omar was captured by an army and taken to the United States where he was enslaved. Omar was originally under the ownership of a cruel owner named Johnson. Said ran away and was later captured and imprisoned for a period of time before eventually ending up under the ownership of Jim Owen, who according to Omar was much more humane. He did not beat Omar or work him harshly. During his time in America, Omar had forgotten much of his original language and Arabic. Omar also became a Christian.

Abdul Rahman was an African prince who had studied at Timbuktu. Much like Said, Abdul Rahman was literate and could write in Arabic. Abdul Rahman was sent abroad by his father to study. Upon returning home, Abdul Rahman joined the army where he became a commander. During a battle in 1787, Abdul Rahman was captured by his enemies, sold into slavery, and was eventually brought to Dominica. From there Abdul Rahman was sold and transferred to another ship that brought him to Mississippi in the United States.

In the United States, Abdul Rahman was bought by a planter named Thomas Foster. Foster also bought Samba, who was a soldier that served under Abdul Rahman. Life on the plantation would prove to be a stark contrast from the life that Abdul Rahman had lived in West Africa. Abdul Rahman offered Foster a ransom for his freedom. This was common in West Africa, but in Mississippi a slave could not attain his freedom so easily and the offer was rejected. Abdul Rahman's long plaited hair was cut, although not without resistance on his part. Abdul Rahman also initially refused to perform the labor that was requested of him, which led to him being whipped. Abdul Rahman made an attempt to run away, but after a number of weeks he was forced to return to Foster's plantation due to the fact that he had nowhere else to stay. Abdul Rahman came to accept his life on the slave plantation, where he was able to distinguish himself due to his unique abilities. In return, Abdul Rahman had enjoyed special privileges on the plantation, such as freedom to continue to practice his Islamic faith. Leaving behind a wife and child in Africa, Abdul Rahman married a slave woman named Isabella and raised a new family.

One day Abdul Rahman happened to encounter Dr. John Cox. Cox was an Irish man that had been marooned while traveling in of Africa. Abdul Rahman provided Cox shelter and nursed him back to health. To show his gratitude to Abdul Rahman, Cox attempted to buy Abdul Rahman's freedom, but Abdul Rahman's owner refused. Cox was willing to pay $1,000 for Abdul Rahman, which was nearly twice the market price for a male slave, but Foster considered Abdul Rahman too valuable a slave to sell. Despite his failure at liberating Abdul Rahman, the two men maintained a friendship until Cox's death in 1816.

Abdul Rahman would get a chance to gain his freedom when he established a friendship with a printer named Andrew Marschalk. In 1826, Marschalk assisted Abdul Rahman with writing a letter to his homeland. The letter was given to Mississippi Senator Thomas Reed, who sent it to Secretary of State Henry Clay. Clay sent the letter to Morocco where it reached the Sultan. The Moroccan Sultan sent a response that reached President John Quincy Adams. President Adams gave his approval for Abdul Rahman to be purchased and in 1828, after forty years of being a slave, Abdul Rahman was liberated.

When Cox attempted to buy Abdul Rahman's freedom, Foster was not willing to release what was his most valuable slave. Foster was now willing to sell Abdul Rahman under the condition that

Abdul Rahman be made to leave the United States. Abdul Rahman returned to Africa, although he never quite made it home. He sailed to Liberia, but he ended up dying there in 1829 at the age of sixty-seven. At the time of his death, Abdul Rahman had hopes of buying his children's freedom so that they could come with him to Africa. The Nation of Islam was in some ways reclaiming the religious practices of at least some of their ancestors by turning to Islam, albeit a much different version of the Islam than Africans like Said and Abdul Rahman would have practiced. Malcolm X himself was aware of the great Islamic civilizations in Africa and the learning center of Timbuktu.

Part of the success of the Nation of Islam in establishing greater pride in black people was that it changed their entire approach towards Africa. The growth of the Nation of Islam was concurrent with the independence movements of Africa, and the connection was very obvious. Malcolm would frequently draw comparisons between the struggles of Africans in the United States with the anti-colonial struggles in Africa. After his break with the Nation of Islam, Malcolm explained: "One of the things that made the Black Muslim movement grow was its emphasis upon things African." Elijah Muhammad had helped to foster links between African Americans and African leaders through activities such as sending Malcolm as his representative to Africa and meeting with Africans such as Amadou Mahtar M'Bow of Senegal.

Although there was an emphasis on Africa within the Nation of Islam, this emphasis often left their followers with a very limited and confused understanding of Africa. The Nation of Islam's mythology stated that black people in America descended from the tribe of a scientist named Shabazz. Shabazz grew angry with the people of Mecca and took his family into the jungles of Africa. So in this mythology black people originated from Arabia, hence the Nation of Islam's rhetoric about the "Asiatic Black Man."

During a discussion on the program *City Desk*, Malcolm explained that Elijah Muhammad had spoken of black people separating and returning "back home." Malcolm seemed to have understood Elijah Muhammad's plans to return back home as meaning an eventual return to Africa. During an address in which Malcolm declared his independence from the Nation of Islam, he explained that he was still a Muslim and he still believed in Elijah Muhammad's teachings on separation. Malcolm explained, "I too believe the best solution is complete separation, with our people going back home, to our own African homeland." Elijah Muhammad himself never really specified what he meant by "back home." Malcolm pointed this out when he declared that Elijah Muhammad "didn't ever say back to Africa." Malcolm explained that Elijah Muhammad was intentionally vague about what he meant by "back home" in order to avoid having to point to a specific geographical location.

After leaving the Nation of Islam and forming his own ideology, Malcolm expressed an even greater interest in Africa. This was an interest that many other black people would come to share, but Elijah Muhammad commented on the growing interest in African culture negatively. In *The Fall of America*, Elijah Muhammad disparaged those black people who were returning to traditional African lifestyles, which Elijah Muhammad described as being uncivilized:

> For nearly forty years I have been preaching to the Black man in America that we should accept our own; and instead of the Black man going to the decent side of his own, he goes back seeking traditional Africa, and the way they did in jungle life and the way you see in some uncivilized parts of Africa today. The Black man in America accepts the jungle life, thinking that they would get the love of Black Africa. Black brother and Black sister, wearing savage dress and hair-styles will not get you the love of Africa. The dignified people of Africa are either Muslim or educated Christians.

Aside from instilling pride in black people and giving them a sense of history, Elijah Muhammad's mythology of Yacub and the creation of white devils also had profound psychological implications. Most of Elijah Muhammad's followers needed no

81

serious convincing to believe his teachings on whites because they had lived through hellish conditions which were caused by white oppression. Those thoughts and feelings were already in the minds of many black people, but the Nation of Islam tapped into those feelings by publicly voicing them. In demonizing white people, Elijah Muhammad also broke the psychological chains that black people had. This reliance on white people is what Malcolm X once referred to as the "white man's disease."

Arguably the greatest symbol of the Nation of Islam's breaking of the mental chains of slavery was the fact that its members rejected their European last names, and typically replaced those names with an X. The Nation of Islam understood that one of the ways through which slaves were stripped of their identity was having their original names replaced by European names. The X was meant to represent the names which black people lost during slavery. Malcolm explained this during a debate at Oxford:

> X is not my real name, but if you study history you'll find why no black man in the Western Hemisphere knows his real name. Some of his ancestors kidnapped our ancestors from Africa, and took us into the Western Hemisphere and sold us there. And our names were stripped from us and so today we don't know who we really are. I am one of those who admit it and so I just put X up there to keep from wearing his name.

Psychologist Amos Wilson explains the power of the mythology of Elijah Muhammad as having a practical impact on his followers. Wilson does not focus on the truthfulness of Elijah Muhammad's religious teachings but on how it shaped the behaviors of his followers; how it inspired them to act in their own self-interest. Wilson explains:

> The idea is not whether Whites are Devils or Angels, but what would happen if we dealt with Whites as if they were Devils. How would that transform our situation as a people? How would that transform our behavior as a people? Would it move us closer to doing for self, would it

> move us closer to controlling our destinies, our own
> behaviors, gaining control of our economies and our
> nations? Would it remove us from being manipulated and
> used by another system? It is not about truth alone; it is
> about self-control. It is about the gaining of power. [...]
> Some of us thought we were doing our "intellectual thing"
> when we got caught up trying to point out his
> "mythologies." Not at all; we must look at function.

What Wilson is saying here is important because Elijah
Muhammad's mythologies provided a very practical foundation to
help his followers understand, cope with, and come up with
solutions to the problems that they faced on a daily basis due to
white supremacy. The Nation of Islam clearly preached a
mythology that slightly resembled the stories in the Bible and the
Quran, but it made itself relevant to the psychological needs of its
followers. Although the Nation of Islam was primarily a religious
organization, it was also an organization that addressed itself to all
of the issues that black people were facing. For this reason Nuri
Tinaz explains that conversion to the Nation of Islam was not a
simple religious conversion:

> It seems inadequate to account for the experiences of those
> who joined the NOI simply as conversion. Their becoming
> members of the NOI and Muslims was not simply a case of
> religious conversion. Rather, it included elements of race,
> ethnicity, nationalism, political awakening and
> consciousness of self and identity.

The Nation of Islam recognized the fact that the activists that were
in favor of integration were being brutalized and jailed simply for
marching for the rights that the constitution had guaranteed for
black people. For this reason the Nation of Islam came to view
marching as a fruitless exercise, and Malcolm, in particular, was
very critical of the famed March on Washington. Malcolm also

harshly criticized Martin Luther King as a "religious Uncle Tom," who was teaching black people to be defenseless. In *The Fall of America*, Elijah Muhammad commented on the fact that Martin Luther King was killed, despite the fact that he was preaching brotherhood with white people:

> Look at what they did to Martin Luther King, a man who was trying to be their brother, a man who publicly taught that he did not want to draw the white man's blood. He said if there was any blood to be spilled, let it be the Black man's blood. His word came true. Poor Man.

Rather than integrating into a society that had brutalized and degraded black people, Elijah Muhammad taught his followers to build for themselves and to rely on themselves. He explained, "To integrate with evil is to be destroyed with evil." This was the function of his mythology. In viewing white people as devils, Elijah Muhammad's followers were able to clearly separate their own self-interests from that of the people that Elijah Muhammad had demonized. This actually has a parallel in the Biblical story of the Hebrews. When the Hebrews escaped from slavery in Egypt, they did not seek to integrate with Egypt or to become Egyptians. They fled Egypt and created a thriving civilization of their own. Malcolm X explained:

> Moses tried to separate his people from Pharaoh, and when he tried, the magicians tried to fool the people into staying with Pharaoh. And we look upon these other organizations that are trying to get Negroes to integrate with this doomed white man as nothing but modern-day magicians, and the Honorable Elijah Muhammad as the modern-day Moses who's trying to separate us from the modern-day Pharaoh.

The Bible's own narrative of the Hebrew people shows that integration had a destructive effect on them. This is why there are repeated warnings against mixing with other people. Deuteronomy 7:3-4 is a warning to the Hebrews against marrying and mixing with other people for they would lead the Hebrews away from their

God and take up the worship of alien gods. In Numbers 25:1-18 we see that Zimri is put to death for taking a Midianite woman. Zimri walked into the assembly with a Midianite woman at the same moment that Moses and Israel's judges were discussing the fact that Moabite women were seducing the men into committing sexual immorality and offering sacrifices to the god Baal. The Midianites were considered to be such a great threat to the Israelites that in Numbers 31 we see that God tells Moses to outright declare war on the Midianites.

This was the reality of the Hebrew people in the Bible. Although they were God's chosen people, they were constantly struggling for survival against outside forces and internal forces as well. Moses returned from Mount Sinai after spending forty days and nights up there to find the Hebrews praying to a golden calf. Outraged by this Moses smashed the ten commandment tablets that God had given him. Moses then melted the calf, grounded it into powder, scattered it on water, and forced the Hebrews to drink it. Exodus 32:27-28 states on that day three thousand people were killed under the orders of Moses. Although God had led the Hebrews out of slavery in Egypt, many of them were still discontented and some were looking to lead the Hebrews away from their covenant with God.

What we have with the Hebrew story is the story of a people struggling to build a nation for themselves in the aftermath of being liberated from centuries of slavery in Egypt. At various times the Hebrews lost faith in God or outright rejected God in favor of alien gods. They engaged in not only military struggles as they fought other tribes in an attempt to conquer Canaan, but they also engaged in an identity struggle as they struggled to maintain their own identity in the face of alien cultures and religions. They were faced with threats from the outside and from within.

The Hebrew story can very clearly be read as a lesson in nation building and in recovering from centuries of slavery. This is why the psychology of the Bible's narratives is so important to the psychology of what Elijah Muhammad accomplished with the

Nation of Islam. Like the Hebrews, black people were a people recovering from slavery while struggling to establish a sense of identity and a sense of nationhood. Not only were they dealing with racist whites that were systematically oppressing them, but also those within the black community that were leading black people astray.

There was a whole message of nation building in the Bible that Elijah Muhammad picked up and blended with some of his own mythologies. Whether or not the teachings were factual did not take away from the fact that those teachings were useful in describing the realities that black people were confronted with. Recognizing that blacks in America were taught to reject themselves and embrace the culture and religious symbols of the very people that were oppressing them, he created the type of organization that demonized all the things that black people were told were superior and in doing so he raised the self-confidence and self-esteem of his followers. He also enabled his followers to create self-sufficient institutions which were not reliant upon the same whites that had oppressed and brutalized black people, much as the Hebrews came to be independent from the Egyptians that had enslaved them.

Despite the achievements of the Nation of Islam in making African Americans more self-reliant and improving their self-confidence, the movement was not without major flaws. The flaws within the Nation of Islam also played into the larger problem of the number of splinter groups that emerged within the original movement. Over the course of the history of the Nation of Islam a number of factions broke from the original movement to create separate (and sometimes rival) Islamic movements.

The earliest of these schisms emerged under Fard Muhammad's leadership. Fard Muhammad taught his followers that they were not Americans and that they had no allegiance to America. One follower named Abdul Muhammad took offense to this and left the organization. He founded his own temple where he stressed loyalty to the United States. This faction did not last very long, however. Similar splinter groups were formed throughout the 1930s by other members.

When Fard Muhammad mysteriously vanished in 1934, Elijah

Muhammad took control of the movement and altered some of Fard's teachings. Fard had appointed Elijah Muhammad to Chief Minister of Islam, which was the second highest position behind Fard, so Elijah Muhammad was the natural successor to Fard. Elijah Muhammad's leadership of the Nation of Islam was not uncontested, however. Many rejected Elijah Muhammad's claim that Fard was Allah. Elijah Muhammad's own brother Kalatt Muhammad was among those who had a dispute with Elijah Muhammad over the new direction of the Nation of Islam. This situation had become so intense that Elijah Muhammad was forced to leave Detroit and went into hiding for seven years. Elijah Muhammad later commented on this situation by explaining:

> In the fall of 1934 most of the followers turned out to be hypocrites and they began to teach against the movement, and to join the enemies of the movement. The situation got so bad that in 1935 it was impossible to go among them because it seemed to me that over 70 percent of them were hypocrites.

One of the most prominent offshoots was the Nation of Gods and Earths. This faction was started by Clarence 13X after he was expelled from the Nation of Islam in 1963. Not only did Clarence differ with the movement when it came to matters of religious belief, but he also enjoyed gambling and drinking, which were both strictly forbidden by the Nation of Islam. Clarence 13X was assassinated in 1969 under mysterious circumstances. Although the identity of his assassin remains unknown, the local press was quick to blame the Nation of Islam for the murder.

Clarence's sect, known as Five Percenters, differed with the Nation of Islam on a number of theological issues. Whereas the Nation of Islam taught that Fard Muhammad was God, Clarence taught his followers that all black men were gods. The term "Five Percenter" is due to Clarence's teachings that 85 percent of humanity believes in a God that does not exist, while another 10 percent are devils that exploit and mislead the majority. The remaining 5 percent are the ones who have been taught the truth and must educate the other 85 percent.

Another prominent offshoot of Elijah Muhammad's organization was the Hanafi Sect. The Hanafi Sect was founded by Hamaas Abdul Khaalis in 1967 as a direct challenge to the Nation of Islam. In 1958 Khaalis left the Nation of Islam, reportedly due to his issues with Elijah Muhammad's spending habits and his private conduct. Khaalis also seemed to have disagreed with Elijah Muhammad's version of Islam, which included the exclusion of whites. It was his introduction to traditional Islam that brought about "a breakdown" in Khaalis' belief in the doctrine of the Nation of Islam. Aside from theological differences there were also political differences. The Hanafi sect expressed more loyalty towards the United States.

The Hanafi Sect came to public attention in 1973 when its headquarters was invaded and seven members of Khaalis' family were murdered. Due to the differences between Khaalis and the Nation of Islam, many felt that the Nation of Islam was behind the murders, despite the denials from Minister Farrakhan. This event may have been retaliation for the fact that Khaalis had sent out letters that denounced Elijah Muhammad as a "lying deceiver" and accused him of promoting false Islam that advocated hatred of whites. In 1977, Khaalis made national news again when he and some of his followers invaded a number of buildings and took hostages. During the hostage negotiation one person was killed.

The most profound split within the original movement was the split between Elijah Muhammad and Malcolm X. This split had multiple repercussions for the Nation of Islam. In losing Malcolm X, the Nation of Islam lost its national spokesman and the movement's most publicly recognized member. Although Elijah Muhammad was the undisputed leader of the movement, it was Malcolm who was the most sought after by the media and the public. Malcolm's popularity was such that Louis Farrakhan would recall that: "Malcolm had become so popular that many writers had felt that Malcolm X was in fact the movement called the Nation of Islam."

Malcolm's popularity was one of the major contributing factors to him being ousted from the movement. There were rumors that Malcolm wanted to take over the Nation of Islam to enrich himself. Malcolm was aware of these rumors, but he ignored them. All Malcolm had to show for his years of service to Elijah Muhammad was a car and house, and he did not outright own either of them. Malcolm had not used his position in the Nation of Islam to enrich himself, but there were some within the movement that did not possess Malcolm's sincerity. These elements in the Nation of Islam were also jealous of Malcolm's fame.

Not only had Malcolm X left the movement, but he became a very vocal critic of the Nation of Islam. He denounced the Nation of Islam as a criminal organization and implicated the movement in the various attempts on his life. He accused Elijah Muhammad of religious fakery for claiming to be the messenger of God and for misusing the religion of Islam for his own purposes. Most damning of all was that Malcolm had exposed that Elijah Muhammad fathered several children out of wedlock. Rumors had been circulating for years that Elijah Muhammad had been carrying on affairs with some of his secretaries and some of those women had even gone to the press to announce that they were filing paternity suits against Elijah Muhammad, but it was not until Malcolm publicly announced this information that such national attention was brought towards Elijah Muhammad's extramarital affairs.

Malcolm's break with the Nation of Islam came after he made the comment that Kennedy's assassination was merely a case of America's chickens coming home to roost. Elijah Muhammad had prohibited his followers from commenting on the assassination and this is precisely what Malcolm X did. He gave a speech titled "God's Judgment of White America." The speech itself avoided the topic of Kennedy's assassination, but during the question and answer period Malcolm was asked a question on Kennedy's assassination to which he responded that it was a case of the chickens coming home to roost.

Malcolm met with Elijah Muhammad shortly after giving his statement on Kennedy and he described the meeting as lacking

Elijah Muhammad's "usual amiability." Instead, there was a tension between the two. It was during this meeting that Elijah Muhammad silenced Malcolm for ninety days as a punishment for his comments on Kennedy. The Nation of Islam also publicly denounced and distanced itself from Malcolm's statements. John Ali publicly read a letter which stated that Malcolm "was speaking for himself and not Muslims in general. And Minister Malcolm has been suspended from public speaking for the time being."

There is a certain irony in the fact that the Nation of Islam, which was so vocal in their rhetoric about "white devils," would silence Malcolm because of statements made about President Kennedy. This of course was actually an excuse to remove Malcolm, as Malcolm himself explained: "Any Muslim would have known that my 'chickens coming home to roost' statement had been only an excuse to put into action the plan for getting me out." Malcolm had previously been very critical of President Kennedy and his administration when he was alive, although Elijah Muhammad seemed to have taken a less critical position of Kennedy. Elijah Muhammad certainly did not endorse or support Kennedy, but he did recognize Kennedy as a president that said some favorable things towards black people and compared Kennedy's assassination with that of Abraham Lincoln:

> From the death of Abraham Lincoln to the assassination of President Kennedy, it proves that on each one of these occasions where outlaws over ruled legal authority, it was in the case of Presidents who opened their mouths and said something favorable for the so-called Negro.

After the ninety days were up, Malcolm was not reinstated. It became obvious to him that he was being forced out of the movement against his will. A contributing factor to this split was the FBI's attempt to create division within the Nation of Islam. An FBI memo from 1969 demonstrated that the FBI had been working on "methods through which the NOI could be discredited in the eyes of the general black populace or through which factionalism among the leadership could be created." The memo goes on to explain that factional disputes were successfully created, the most notable of which was Malcolm X. There was a very clear divide and conquer plan at play here, and the Nation of Islam seemed to have played into it very well by publicly denouncing and criticizing Malcolm. Malcolm initially planned to ignore the Nation of Islam after he left the movement. He certainly had no intentions of criticizing the movement and expressed regret that he was even maneuvered into a situation where he was at odds with his former organization. Malcolm explained:

> The situation I have been maneuvered into right now between me and the Black Muslim movement is something that I really deeply regret, because I don't think anything is more destructive than two groups of Black people fighting each other.

In an attempt to quell some of tensions between his organization and the Nation of Islam, Malcolm sent a letter to Elijah Muhammad in which Malcolm pleaded that "we should be working in unity with other leaders and organisations in an effort to solve the very serious problems facing all Afro-Americans." The letter failed to ease the tensions, however. Within the Nation of Islam, Malcolm was depicted as a hypocrite and a traitor for denouncing Elijah Muhammad. Muhammad Ali, a former friend of Malcolm, declared that: "Mr. (Elijah) Muhammad will destroy him through Allah. You just don't buck Mr. Muhammad and get away with it." Although Malcolm was a close friend of Muhammad Ali and helped bring him into the movement at a time when the Nation of Islam attempted to distance itself from the boxer, Ali's loyalty was very clearly with Elijah Muhammad. It was understood in the Nation of Islam that anyone that defied Elijah Muhammad would be punished and Malcolm was no different. Elijah Muhammad fostered this type of thinking among his followers. Dr A. Salaam explained that Elijah Muhammad had told his followers:

> When people attack me those of you around me you should

defend me. I don't have to go out after them myself. It is not dignified for me to chase them. But you are my followers and ministers, you should not allow people to attack your leader.

The situation between Malcolm and Ali is particularly worth noting given the fact that Malcolm was supporting Ali at a time when the Nation of Islam had distanced themselves from Ali. The Nation of Islam decried professional sports and refused to cover sporting events in their newspapers. Once Ali had defeated Sonny Liston and became the champion, the Nation of Islam's views had changed and he was subsequently embraced by the movement and given the name Muhammad Ali by Elijah Muhammad—Ali's name had previously been Cassius Clay. Thus the same organization that condemned boxing now publicly embraced a boxer. There were other contradictions in this as well, such as the fact that Ali's trainer was Angelo Dundee, a white man. The Nation of Islam taught their followers to eat only once a day, yet Ali broke this teaching.

A number of people commented on the Nation of Islam's embrace of Ali with sarcasm and skepticism. One commentator stated that the Nation of Islam "thought sports was a mortal sin till Cassius came along." Another source stated, "They're getting a lot of mileage out of him now, but they'll drop him like a hot potato when he's outlived his usefulness to them." Malcolm himself noted: "I don't know if the champion today cares to remember that most newspapers in America were represented at the pre-fight camp—except *Muhammad Speaks*. Even though Cassius was a Muslim brother, the Muslim newspaper didn't consider his fight worth covering."

Much of this change in attitude must have been related to the fame and prestige that Ali brought to the Nation of Islam. The loss of Malcolm left the Nation of Islam without a prominent national spokesman. Elijah Muhammad was the leader of the organization, but his following outside of the Nation of Islam was very limited. Like Malcolm, Ali had an appeal and popularity in the black community that went beyond Elijah Muhammad, and the fact that Ali had credited his victories in the ring to Islam and the teachings of Elijah Muhammad kept the movement in the spotlight and attracted new followers. Jeremiah Shabazz explained as much when he stated:

> When Elijah Muhammad spoke, his words were confined to whatever city he had spoken in. But Ali was a sports hero, and people wanted to know what he had to say, so his visibility and prominence were of great benefit to the Nation. His voice carried throughout the world, and that was a true blessing for us. There's no doubt, our following increased enormously, maybe a hundred percent, after he joined the Nation.

When Malcolm was assassinated, the Nation of Islam did not mourn or even acknowledge the role that some Muslims played in Malcolm's assassination. Elijah Muhammad accused Malcolm of "mudslinging" and declared: "We didn't want to kill Malcolm and we didn't try to kill him. They know I didn't harm Malcolm. They know I loved him. His foolish teaching brought him to his own end." Elijah Muhammad denied having any involvement in Malcolm's death and instead accused Malcolm of being a "hypocrite" who tried to make "war" against him and he portrayed Malcolm's death as being of Malcolm's own doing. In pretending that Malcolm brought this fate upon himself, Elijah Muhammad had purposefully ignored the fact that some of his own followers were involved in Malcolm's assassination and that the Nation of Islam had engaged in rhetoric that seemed to have endorsed having Malcolm killed. For example, in one of his speeches, Farrakhan claimed that by criticizing Elijah Muhammad, Malcolm was "asking for death" and that Malcolm "got what he asked for." He also praised Malcolm's murderers as "fearless men" for killing Malcolm in front of his followers. Far from mourning the senseless murder of a man that contributed greatly to the Nation of Islam's development, the leaders within the Nation of Islam practically celebrated Malcolm's death.

The irony is that for all the criticisms made of Malcolm for being a hypocrite and a traitor, even after leaving the Nation of Islam, Malcolm remained more loyal to the movement than many who were within the Nation of Islam. Malcolm pointed this out when he declared that the Nation of Islam was "thoroughly infiltrated." Malcolm had received a visit from the FBI in which they tried to pay him off in return for information about the Nation of Islam. Malcolm refused, but others did not have the same loyalty to Elijah Muhammad. John Ali, the national Secretary for the Nation of Islam, was an FBI informant, and there were surely more informants in the movement. There were others that saw Malcolm's ouster as an opportunity to advance their own position in the Nation of Islam. Louis Farrakhan, a man who was once a friend and associate of Malcolm's, seemed to have been one of those people. When Malcolm left the Nation of Islam, Farrakhan became one of Malcolm's biggest detractors and critics. Not only did Farrakhan's rank in the movement elevate after Malcolm's departure and subsequent assassination, but some of Farrakhan's children had married relatives of Elijah Muhammad. Elijah Muhammad himself seemed to have grown cautious of Farrakhan's intentions, as Elijah Muhammad Jr. recalls: "My father told me to keep an eye on him because he was trying to use the family." Farrakhan had also apparently been having secret meetings in which he was trying to convince other Muslims that he would be Elijah Muhammad's successor.

An even greater irony than the abovementioned one is that the Nation of Islam had, at times, worked with the Ku Klux Klan and the American Nazi Party. Malcolm himself represented the Nation of Islam in meetings with the Klan. These connections to white supremacists were among the things that Malcolm would publicly criticize Elijah Muhammad for after he left the movement. It is curious that for all the ties the Nation of Islam had to white supremacists, they viciously denounced Malcolm more so than they did the same white supremacists that they had worked with. The Nation of Islam had no problem inviting the likes of George Lincoln Rockwell to their rallies and even allowed him to speak, but when Malcolm left the movement he quickly became the main target of scorn for the Nation of Islam. Not only was Malcolm a target, but others that had left the movement or showed any type of loyalty to Malcolm became targets as well, and were often brutalized. For all their rhetoric about "white devils," the Nation of Islam never confronted white supremacists with the same force they used against "traitors" within the organization. Malcolm himself pointed this out when he explained, "The Black Muslim movement has never at any time been involved in any kind of strike against the Ku Klux Klan or the Citizens' Council. Even in the South or the North. But they give the orders to fight each other."

Creating division within the Nation of Islam proved to be particularly easy due to the structure of the organization. Elijah Muhammad, who was considered the messenger of God, was at the head of the organization and loyalty to him was strict and absolute. Wallace Deen Muhammad, the son and successor of Elijah Muhammad, explained that to charge Elijah Muhammad with a serious allegation such as infidelity or adultery meant that "somebody might kill you in the Nation of Islam." Perhaps even more so than Wallace Muhammad, Malcolm understood the degree of loyalty that Muslims had to Elijah Muhammad and the dangers involved in accusing Elijah Muhammad of hypocrisy. Malcolm explained, "if someone came to me and I had no knowledge whatsoever of what had taken place and they told me what I'm saying, I would kill them myself. The only thing that would prevent me from killing someone who made a statement like this, they would have to be able to let me know that it's true." What Malcolm is referring to here were the rumors that Elijah Muhammad had fathered children with his secretaries out of wedlock.

Elijah Muhammad preached a strict moral code and under the rules of the Nation of Islam anyone who committed adultery was suspended from the movement, and very often humiliated as well. Malcolm had been forced to reject his own brother because he was carrying on improper relations with a secretary. It was for these reasons that Elijah Muhammad's infidelities were a blow to

Malcolm's faith in Elijah Muhammad. Although Malcolm was disappointed that Elijah Muhammad had fathered children out of wedlock, Malcolm was willing to forgive his teacher. Malcolm reasoned: "David's adultery with Bathsheba weighed less on history's scales, for instance, than the positive fact of David's killing Goliath." Malcolm also took it upon himself to inform other ministers to help prepare them for the challenges this revelation would bring to the Nation of Islam. Malcolm found that some of them had already known the situation, including Minister Louis Farrakhan, then known as Louis X.

At the time Malcolm took a position that prepared him to defend Elijah Muhammad, but over time, as his dedication to Elijah Muhammad faded, Malcolm became critical of the acts of his teacher. Later speaking on the morality of Elijah Muhammad, Malcolm explained that his biggest issue with Elijah Muhammad's actions was that he tried to hide what he had done rather than owning up to it:

> You can't take nine teenaged women and seduce them and give them babies and then tell me you're moral. You could do it if you admitted you did it and admitted that the babies were yours. I'd shake your hand and call you a man. A good one too. But any time you seduce teenaged girls and make them be charged with adultery, make them hide your crimes, why, you're not even a man, much less a divine man.

Malcolm did not initially intend to publicly denounce Elijah Muhammad in such a manner, but he was under increasing stress from repeated attempts on his life. When Malcolm's house was firebombed, Malcolm was convinced that the Nation of Islam had carried out the bombing under the orders of Elijah Muhammad. The organization certainly expressed no concern or condolences for the attack. In fact, the Nation of Islam accused Malcolm of starting the fire himself. To this Malcolm responded, "if anybody can find where I've bombed my house, they can put a rifle bullet through my head. It was my children and my own life and my wife's life that was at stake."

Malcolm became very fatalistic about his situation and had accepted that he would soon be assassinated, most likely at the hands of Muslims, explaining: "I have said publicly many times that I know that they have their orders. Anyone who chooses not to believe what I am saying doesn't know the Muslims in the Nation of Islam." According to Alex Haley, Malcolm had been hearing that he was "a marked man" from members of the Nation of Islam. Understanding that nothing is done in the Nation of Islam without the approval of Elijah Muhammad, Malcolm naturally saw the hand of his former teacher in all of the public attacks that were being launched against him by the Nation of Islam. Moreover, Malcolm himself also understood how the Nation of Islam operated and treated those who were considered traitors or threats to the movement. Malcolm was convinced that the Nation of Islam was trying to kill him, although he had privately told Alex Haley that he felt forces that were more powerful than the Nation of Islam were also trying to silence him.

Elijah Muhammad denied any involvement in Malcolm's murder, although, privately he seemed to have welcomed the idea of Malcolm being killed. In 1964, the FBI recorded a private conversation between Elijah Muhammad and an "unknown individual" where Elijah Muhammad had viciously denounced Malcolm. He told the unknown person that he would throw out anyone who was found supporting Malcolm and that Malcolm should be left to stay outside the Nation of Islam until he rots. Referring to Malcolm as "that no good long-legged Malcolm," Elijah Muhammad explained that the only way to deal with Malcolm was to get rid of him the way that "Moses and others did their bad ones." Elijah Muhammad also mentioned that hypocrites should have their heads cut off. Although not directly calling for Malcolm's death in this conversation, the implications of what Elijah Muhammad was saying was very clear. Malcolm was a hypocrite who, in the words of Farrakhan, was "worthy of death."

Although Elijah Muhammad had taught his followers not to act violently unless they were attacked and his followers were prohibited from carrying firearms, Malcolm was certainly well-aware that members of the Nation of Islam could act violently towards perceived threats. Leon Ameer, who was a member of the Nation of Islam, was viciously attacked and beaten by members of the Nation of Islam. Likewise, Aubrey Barnette was also assaulted for leaving the Nation of Islam. Prior to Malcolm's death, there were also multiple attempts made on his life. Malcolm had identified the people who had attempted to kill him as Muslims.

As mentioned before, Malcolm had privately expressed doubts as to whether or not the Nation of Islam was truly behind everything that was happening to him. Others shared similar doubts about the role of the Nation of Islam in Malcolm's assassination. Wallace Deen Muhammad explained: "I don't think the Nation of Islam planned the assassination of Malcolm X. I assume outsiders assassinated Malcolm X but Muslims were used." James Farmer stated that he did not think that Elijah Muhammad and the Nation of Islam "had anything to do with his [Malcolm's] killing." Malcolm's half-sister Ella Collins explained that Malcolm himself had expressed the view that the firebombing of his house was much bigger than the Nation of Islam and that she felt Malcolm's assassination was also bigger than the Nation of Islam. Nuri Tinaz conducted interviews with several Muslims and all of them claimed that Elijah Muhammad had never ordered anyone to kill Malcolm. They said that Elijah Muhammad had told them "leave him [Malcolm] alone…this between him and Allah."

The reality was that Malcolm was not left alone. He was viciously denounced by a number of Elijah Muhammad's supporters. Elijah Muhammad's own son, Elijah Muhammad Jr., was said to have publicly declared to the Fruit of Islam that Malcolm should be killed and have his tongue mailed to Chicago. There was also a plot to wire a bomb in Malcolm's car on the part of some of the Muslims. Elijah Muhammad's own private statements about Malcolm made it very clear that Malcolm was considered a traitor and deserved death. If the leadership within the Nation of Islam did not order Malcolm's assassination, they certainly created the atmosphere that contributed not only to Malcolm's murder, but the violent attacks on those who had left the Nation of Islam.

The question of who really killed Malcolm is a complicated one that will not be dealt with here, but what is important for the purposes of this essay is that the structure of the Nation of Islam and Elijah Muhammad's private conduct not only made creating divisions in the movement easy, but it also caused a particularly bitter split between Elijah Muhammad and Malcolm X. Elijah Muhammad came to view Malcolm as a hypocrite and a traitor to the Nation of Islam. Malcolm, on the other hand, would publicly denounce his former teacher as an immoral religious faker. The result of this was an atmosphere that led fanatics within the Nation of Islam to assassinate Malcolm.

Malcolm's assassination did not quell the dissatisfaction within the Nation of Islam and much of the growing dissatisfaction mirrored many of the criticisms that Malcolm X had made of the movement. One of the criticisms that Malcolm raised was Elijah Muhammad's increasing focus on monetary wealth. Malcolm had noticed that after Elijah Muhammad returned from a visit to the Middle East the entire direction of the Nation of Islam began to change. The organization became less militant and Malcolm explained that Elijah Muhammad became more interested in acquiring wealth and money. A growing segment of the Nation of Islam became frustrated with the wealth that Elijah Muhammad had amassed for himself. They began to feel exploited by the Nation of Islam because it was their salaries that were paying for the wealth that Elijah Muhammad and his family enjoyed, which included the expensive houses that Elijah Muhammad and his family lived in.

There were also a growing number of violent clashes within the Nation of Islam. Although Elijah Muhammad strictly prohibited his followers from carrying arms and engaging in unprovoked acts of violence, the murder of Malcolm X clearly highlighted the fact there were extreme elements within the Nation of Islam that were willing to kill. Many of these same elements took to killing other Muslims to express their frustrations. During this period a number of dissident groups emerged within the Nation of Islam. This would also signal the trend of splinter groups that would only increase in the aftermath of Elijah Muhammad's death.

One of these dissident groups, known as the Young Muslims, carried out a series of killings of more conservative members of the organization. Among their victims was Raymond Sharrieff, the son-in-law of Elijah Muhammad, whom they had attempted to kill. The Young Muslims were upset with the fact that Elijah Muhammad had amassed such a large personal fortune for himself and his family. They wanted to see equal wealth distribution in the movement, but their attempt to express these criticisms directly to Elijah Muhammad was blocked by officials within the organization.

Two splinter movements that emerged in the early 1970s were the New World of Islam and Calistran. Both groups were critical of the Nation of Islam because in their view the Nation of Islam was not militant and uncompromising enough. Like the other activists and Black Nationalists, the New World of Islam criticized the Nation of Islam for not doing more to challenge the status quo. In doing so, the New World of Islam organized demonstrations against the white establishment and directly confronted the police. One branch of this organization also targeted the Nation of Islam, including killing James Shabazz, who was a local minister of Temple No. 25 in New Jersey.

The Calistran sought to earn an elite status known as Death Angels by killing a certain number of "devils." To join the group, one had to kill four white children, five white women or nine white men. In October 1973 there were fifteen Death Angels in California that were responsible for the killings of over 200 white people throughout the state. The Calistran had taken Elijah Muhammad's teachings of white people being devils to a deadlier level by resorting to killing whites in order to establish a Muslim dominated city.

Malcolm had accused the Nation of Islam of becoming a criminal organization and the latter years of Elijah Muhammad's leadership of the organization confirmed what Malcolm was saying. The Nation of Islam in many ways did become a criminal organization, though not by design. These acts of violence and murder were against the general teachings of the Nation of Islam, which had advocated violence only in self-defense if one was threatened and Elijah Muhammad prohibited the carrying of firearms. These various dissident groups were harshly denounced by the Nation of Islam. Elijah Muhammad proclaimed in an issue of *Muhammad Speaks* that "while trying to make unity, the Muslims are faced with murderers and killers coming to them from among our Black brothers."

The chaos that ensued in the post-Malcolm years of the Nation of Islam is marked by the fact that in many ways Malcolm had predicted this. Malcolm explained that "today the reason you have so much incidence of Muslim attacking Muslim is because the spiritual force that used to exist in the movement, among the rank and file is gone." Malcolm further charged that Elijah Muhammad did not love black people because he refused to do anything about the numerous acts of violence that his own followers were engaged in. Indeed, Elijah Muhammad did help to contribute to the violence by encouraging the rhetoric about "traitors" and "hypocrites." Elijah Muhammad never publicly called for violence against the perceived enemies of the Nation of Islam, but, as the FBI recorded conversation shows, Elijah Muhammad was privately using incendiary and violent language to describe Malcolm and all others that had left the Nation of Islam. Elijah Muhammad also never condemned the rhetoric some of his own ministers had been using to describe Malcolm and other "traitors."

When Elijah Muhammad died in 1975, in a sense so too did his movement. Elijah Muhammad never appointed an official successor. It was assumed that Malcolm X would have been the next successor, but Malcolm's break from the movement created a leadership void in the organization. Further complicating the issue over succession of leadership was that Elijah Muhammad, who was appointed as the messenger by Fard Muhammad, felt that it was not his place to appoint a successor. He felt that since Allah had selected him, only Allah could select his successor. Elijah Muhammad's son Wallace Muhammad ended up taking control of the movement. Wallace had deep disagreements with his father's teachings, however. Wallace began bringing the Nation of Islam closer towards Sunni Islam, eventually changing the name of the original Nation of Islam to the American Society of Muslims. Malcolm had stated in his autobiography that Wallace held the conviction that "the only possible salvation for the Nation of Islam would be its accepting and projecting a better understanding of Orthodox Islam."

Wallace set about dismantling and restructuring the movement, which included relaxing some of the strict policies of the Nation of Islam. Some of these changes created divisions within Wallace's organization. Unlike the original organization, Wallace was not very critical of America's racism or injustices. Wallace's political views alienated many within his organization. One Muslim stated: "Most of my colleagues and I became dissatisfied with Imam W. D. Mohammed's politics. Because he is so close to American political establishments." There were also others that remained faithful to Elijah Muhammad's original teachings, such as Farrakhan.

Louis Farrakhan broke with Wallace Muhammad and then revived the Nation of Islam in 1977. Farrakhan revived many of Elijah Muhammad's teachings and ideas. Although Farrakhan revived the Nation of Islam and achieved much of the national prominence of the original movement, the split within the original movement persisted, and a number of splinter organizations have claimed to be the true successors to Elijah Muhammad's movement. Some of the other organizations have included the United Nation of Islam founded by Abass Rassoull, a separate organization also called the Nation of Islam led by Elijah Muhammad's older brother John Muhammad, and the Lost-Found Nation of Islam founded by Silis Muhammad.

It is interesting to consider what direction Elijah Muhammad would have taken the Nation of Islam in had he lived longer. The Nation of Islam had made a number of prophecies about the impending destruction of America and the liberation of black people. For instance, Elijah Muhammad had prophesied that the fall of America was to come during 1965 and 1966, but this never occurred. Dr. Salaam noted that Elijah Muhammad began to grow suspicious of these prophecies. Elijah Muhammad's position on whites also seemed to be changing. In his last public speech Elijah Muhammad told black people to stop blaming white people and start placing the blame for their situation on themselves. Moreover, Elijah Muhammad spoke of having his followers prove to white Muslims that they are "Muslim at heart." A number of Muslims commented on the fact that in this final speech, Elijah Muhammad was teaching something that differed from his old messages.

It cannot be overlooked that the Nation of Islam reformed many black people and gave them a new sense of self-worth and identity. Even some of the people at the lowest segment of society, such as drug addicts and prostitutes, were reformed and changed by the message of the Nation of Islam. The organization also brought back Garvey's concept of self-reliance and nation building. Those were the strengths of the movement, yet it also cannot be overlooked that the Nation of Islam was plagued by some major issues as well. Elijah Muhammad's private conduct and his personal wealth became a source of division and controversy within the movement. The growing corruption and economic mismanagement within the Nation of Islam eventually led to a series of violent clashes that resulted in the deaths of many Muslims. The life of Malcolm X may very well be a summary of the best and the worst of the Nation of Islam. The organization helped to shape him into the influential leader that he became, yet Malcolm's critiques of the flaws within the organization proved to be prophetic.

Selected References:

Alex Haley and Malcolm X, *The Autobiography of Malcolm X*, (1965).

Alex Kronemer, Louis Barbash, and Michael Wolfe, "Prince Among Slaves: A Documentary Film Project," *Southern Quarterly*, 2007.

Amos Wilson, *The Falsification of Afrikan Consciousness: Eurocentric History, Psychiatry and the Politics of White Supremacy*, (Afrikan World InfoSystems, 1993).

Andy Newman and John Eligon, "Killer of Malcolm X is Granted Parole," *New York Times*, March 19, 2010.

David Jackson, "Ascent And Grandeur: Nurtured By The Nation Of Islam, Schooled In Its Tangle Of Intrigues, Louis Farrakhan Emerges Triumphant As Elijah Muhammad's Successor And An Empire Builder," *Chicago Tribune*, March 15, 1995.

Elijah Muhammad, *The Fall of America*, 1973.

Keith V. Erickson, "Black Messiah: The Father Divine Peace Mission Movement," *Quarterly Journal of Speech*, Volume 63, December 1977.

George Breitman (Editor), *Malcolm X Speaks*

Malcolm X, Arnold Perl (director), 1972. Film

Maureen Smith, "*Muhammad Speaks* and Muhammad Ali: Intersections of the Nation of Islam and Sport in the 1960s" *International Sports Studies*, Volume 22, 2000.

Muhammad, Nafeesa Haniyah, "Perceptions and Experiences in Elijah Muhammad's Economic Program: Voices from the

Pioneers" (2010). *African-American Studies Theses*

Nun Tinaz, "Conversion of African Americans to Islam: A Sociological Analysis of the Nation of Islam And Associated Groups" University of Warwick, February 2001 (dissertation).

Omar ibn Said, *Autobiography of Omar ibn Said*, 1831.

Steven Barboza, "About Men; My Conversation," *New York Times*, April 24, 1994.

Tony Martin, *Race First: The Ideological and Organizational Struggles*, (The Majority Press, 1986).

3

IDA B. WELLS-BARNETT: A NEGLECTED WOMAN IN THE AFRO-AMERICAN STRUGGLE

The life of Ida Bell Wells-Barnett is an interesting one. She was born a slave during the Civil War in 1862 and during her adult life she worked as a contemporary of leaders such as Frederick Douglass, Booker T. Washington, W.E.B. Du Bois, and Marcus Garvey. She is best known for being a leading and courageous opponent of lynchings. In various pamphlets Wells-Barnett documented and exposed lynchings across the United States. Her anti-crusading led Wells-Barnett on a tour across Great Britain to win support for the anti-lynching cause. Despite these accomplishments, Wells-Barnett comes across as an often forgotten and neglected person in the fight against lynching and racism. During her lifetime her efforts were increasingly overshadowed by other activists, particularly by the National Association for the Advancement of Colored People (NAACP). This was something that seemed to have bothered her later in her life.

Much of this neglect was due to the fact that Wells-Barnett's ideology never fit comfortably with any of the contemporary leaders of her time. She was an advocate of self-reliance much as Booker T. Washington and Marcus Garvey were, but she was one of the leading critics of Washington, and she was very suspicious and critical of Garvey's goals. Wells-Barnett was closely aligned with the NAACP, but problems between her and certain people in that organization prevented her from working with them. She particularly had issues with W.E.B. Du Bois. The result was that during her lifetime she worked alongside some of the most prominent African American leaders and organizations, but she was never able to truly work with them.

The biggest obstacle that Wells-Barnett faced as a national leader was Booker T. Washington. Her tense relationship with him would cast a shadow over her involvement as an activist because of the influence that Washington exerted within the black community, especially the press. Despite becoming one of Washington's most prominent critics, Wells-Barnett and Washington did share the common view that African Americans had to be self-sufficient and they preached economic self-help. Wells-Barnett expressed these views when she declared:

> Let the Afro-American depend on no party, but on himself for his salvation. Let him continue to education, character, and above all, put money in his purse. When he has a dollar in his pocket and many more in the bank, he can move from injustice and oppression and no one to say him nay. When he has money, and plenty of it, parties and races will become his servants.

Where the two differed was that Wells-Barnett did not believe in the accommodation of Jim Crow like Washington did. Unlike Washington, Wells-Barnett held the view that yielding to whites would not benefit black people. She declared: "The more the Afro-American yields and cringes and begs, the more he has to do so, the more he is insulted, outraged and lynched." These views were no doubt influenced by the fact that Wells-Barnett had three friends—Thomas Moss, Calvin McDowell, and Henry Stewart—that were lynched. Those three were among those who believed that the "the problem was to be solved by eschewing politics and putting money in the purse." The sad irony is that they were killed precisely because of their economic success. The three of them operated a successful grocery store and the success of the grocery store threatened a local white grocer. For Wells-Barnett economic empowerment was a means to an end in the struggle to overcome discrimination and Jim Crow. She explained, "The appeal to the white man's pocket has ever been more effectual than all the appeals ever made to his conscience. Nothing, absolutely nothing, is to be gained by a further sacrifice of manhood and self-respect." Therefore, she saw economic empowerment as a means to influence the self-interest of white people.

Washington's approach was much more conservative than Wells-Barnett's. Washington was not someone who would denounce white racism or the oppression of African people in public, regardless of how he felt in private. This was also true of Washington's treatment of colonialism in Africa. During a trip to Berlin in 1910, Washington spoke very favorably about German colonialism in Togo. Washington stated that the Germans "do not seek to repress the Africans, but rather to help them that they may be more useful to themselves and to the German people."

Wells-Barnett, unlike Washington, was an advocate of militant forms of self-defense. She declared that "a Winchester rifle should have a place of honor in every black home, and it should be used for that protection which the law refuses to give." This is also demonstrated by Wells-Barnett's support of Robert Charles, who was vilified in the white press. Robert Charles was with a nineteen year old named Leonard Pierce sitting on doorsteps speaking when they were confronted by police officers who attempted to arrest them. One of the officers put a gun to Pierce's face, while officer Mora attacked Charles with a billy club. In the ensuing conflict, Charles drew his gun and fired a shot. Both he and the police officer were wounded, with Mora getting the worse of the two. Charles managed to escape, while Pierce was taken to the police station.

According to Ida Wells-Barnett, Charles "very bravely determined to protect his life as long as he had breath in his body and strength to draw a hair trigger on his would-be murderers. How well he was justified in that belief is well shown by the newspaper accounts which were given of this transaction. Without a single line of evidence to justify the assertion, the New Orleans daily papers at once declared that both Pierce and Charles were desperadoes, that they were contemplating a burglary and that they began the assault upon the policemen."

Following the initial confrontation between Charles and the officer, there was a large manhunt for Charles. Charles, who was a skilled shot, was a difficult target for the police. They managed to surround Charles' home, but Charles' deadly aim resulted in the death of two of the officers. The manhunt came to an end when

Charles was cornered in a small building. As the mob approached to kill him, Charles continued to fire shots at them, killing and wounding many people.

Wells-Barnett describes Charles' final moments as follows:

> Unable to get to him in his stronghold, the besiegers set fire to his house of refuge. While the building was burning Charles was shooting, and every crack of his death-dealing rifle added another victim to the price which he had placed upon his own life. Finally, when fire and smoke became too much for flesh and blood to stand, the long sought for fugitive appeared in the door, rifle in hand, to charge the countless guns that were drawn upon him. With a courage which was indescribable, he raised his gun to fire again, but this time it failed, for a hundred shots riddled his body, and he fell dead face fronting to the mob.

By the end of the manhunt, Charles had killed seven people; four of which were police officers. Eight others were seriously wounded, while twelve others were slightly wounded. In all, Charles had shot twenty-seven white people. Despite the attempts by the press to vilify Charles, Wells-Barnett wrote of him:

> So he lived and so he would have died had not he raised his hand to resent unprovoked assault and unlawful arrest that fateful Monday night. That made him an outlaw, and being a man of courage he decided to die with his face to the foe. The white people of this country may charge that he was a desperado, but to the people of his own race Robert Charles will always be regarded as the hero of New Orleans.

Both Washington and Wells-Barnett relied on the support of white people, but towards two different ends. Washington relied on white philanthropy to fund and support his program at Tuskegee, whereas Wells-Barnett sought to manipulate the self-interest of whites to her favor. Believing that the "white man's dollar is his god," Wells-Barnett took the position that in order to end the "outrages" African Americans had to properly exercise their economic power to "effect a bloodless revolution."

Wells-Barnett also frequently addressed white audiences in hope of winning their support. In 1894 and 1895, Wells-Barnett traveled around the country speaking mainly to white audiences. Wells-Barnett also went to Britain on a tour to promote her anti-lynching campaign. Wells-Barnett hoped that the British could exert their influence to help end lynching, much like Britain's past anti-slavery campaign. Wells-Barnett also sought to target the white press. She was disappointed to find that the northern white press had not picked up on her anti-lynching writings "since it was the medium through which I hoped to reach the white people of the country, who alone could mold public sentiment." For Wells-Barnett, the key to winning white support for her anti-lynching campaign was to re-educate them. As she explained: "We must educate the white people out of their 250 years of slave history."

Another key difference was over their view of industrial education. Washington was a staunch advocate of industrial training for African Americans as a means of bettering their condition, but Wells-Barnett criticized this approach. She pointed out that industrial work was just about the only thing African Americans had actually been trained for:

> The gospel of work is no new one for the Negro. It is the South's old slavery practice in a new dress. It was the only education the South gave the Negro for two and a half centuries she had absolute control of his body and soul.

Moreover, Wells-Barnett was critical of Washington's solution to lynching:

> Mr. Washington says in substance: Give me money to educate the Negro and when he is taught how to work, he will not commit the crime for which lynching is done. Mr. Washington knows when he says this that lynching is not invoked to punish crime but color, and not even industrial

education will change that.

We see some ideological similarities between Washington and Wells-Barnett, but there were also differences that led Wells-Barnett to criticize Washington's approach to dealing with racial problems. Wells-Barnett first contacted Washington in November 1890, when she commended his "manly criticism of our corrupt and ignorant ministry." She and her husband also maintained close ties with Thomas T. Fortune, who was himself a close friend of Washington's.

In 1900, Washington launched the National Negro Business League to compete with the Afro-American Council. Wells-Barnett wrote an editorial in the *Conservator* in which she claimed that the new organization would draw away resources from the business bureau that the Afro-American Council established. Wells-Barnett commented that Washington "will not go anywhere or do anything unless he is 'the whole Thing.' He can't be 'all in all' in the Council for there are others who are as anxious as he is to find the right, and equally anxious to do it." She also accused Washington of wanting to form an organization where he would be "president, moderator, and dictator." Washington expressed his displeasure with this by stating: "Miss Wells is fast making herself so ridiculous that everybody is getting tired of her."

Wells-Barnett was not wrong in her criticisms of Washington, however. Washington was the type of person who exercised a firm control over the black press and worked to silence any dissenting voices in the community. For example, in 1908, Washington bought the *Conservator* newspaper. Washington had in fact bought a number of black owned newspapers. Wells-Barnett's criticisms of Washington also alienated her from Washington's supporters, many of whom held influential positions in the very organizations that Wells-Barnett worked with.

Thomas Holt explains that "Wells-Barnett belonged to the Du Bois-NAACP camp ideologically, but in the end her relations with her allies were not much better than were her relations with

Washington." Like Wells-Barnett, Du Bois was critical of Washington. This was expressed in the essay he wrote on Booker T. Washington in his book *The Souls of Black Folk*. Du Bois notes the many of Washington's achievements, including his securing the financial support of southern whites, but Du Bois also explained that Washington "insists on thrift and self-respect, but at the same time counsels a silent submission to civic inferiority such as is bound to sap the manhood of any race in the long run." Du Bois pointed out that Washington simultaneously criticized the South's lynchings of black people, yet he also held a position that seemed to state that the South's attitude towards black people was "justified" because of the degradation of black people in the South.

Wells-Barnett wrote of this conflict between the two and explained that a large number of people side with Du Bois:

> Although the country at large seemed to be accepting and adopting Mr. Washington's theories of industrial education, a large number agreed with Dr. Du Bois that it was impossible to limit the aspirations and endeavors of an entire race within the confines of the industrial education program.

The NAACP was formed as an organization that took the position that advancement for African Americans would only be attained through political agitation and protesting, rather than Washington's model of economic advancement and industrial training as a means to liberate African Americans. The formation of the NAACP presents yet another example of Wells-Barnett's difficulties in working within organizations. Du Bois explained that Wells-Barnett "refused to join the new organization, being distrustful of white leadership." Wells-Barnett's explanation for why she did not join the NAACP differs from Du Bois, however. According to Wells-Barnett's account of the situation, Du Bois was the one who was directly involved in her not becoming a member of the organization.

Leading up to the creation of the NAACP, a Committee of 40 was selected. Wells-Barnett was confident that she would be among the list of 40 people, but when Du Bois had finished reading the list her name had not been called. Wells-Barnett immediately got up to leave. Her friend John Milholland stopped her before she left the building and expressed his disbelief that she could be left off of the list given her "battle against lynching."

Wells-Barnett blamed Du Bois for her removal. Du Bois himself admitted to having removed Wells-Barnet's name, but he did so with the understanding that she would still be represented in the NAACP through Celia Woolley. Woolley was the founder of the Frederick Douglass Center, of which Wells-Barnett was vice-president. Du Bois was unaware that relations between Wells-Barnett and the Douglass Center were strained at the time, however. Regardless, Du Bois used this as an excuse to justify switching Wells-Barnett's name for Dr. Charles E. Bentley.

Du Bois offered to put Wells-Barnett back on the list, but Wells-Barnett refused. She was so angry at Du Bois that Wells-Barnett explained she did a "foolish thing" by leaving the building and failing to recognize the work of the white men to "rectify" what Du Bois had done. It is interesting that Du Bois mentioned none of this in his account and makes it appear as though Wells-Barnett refused to join the NAACP out of her distrust of white leadership, when in Wells-Barnett's own autobiography she pointed out that the white men in the NAACP seemed to have appreciated her more so than Du Bois did.

Wells-Barnett ultimately regretted not being more involved with the NAACP. She wrote:

> I cannot resist the conclusion that, had I not been so hurt over the treatment I received at the hands of the men of my own race and thus blinded to the realization that I should have taken the place which the white men of the committee felt I should have, the NAACP would now be a live, active force in the lives of our people all over this country.

Wells-Barnett's relationship with the NAACP was an uneasy one. Wells-Barnett criticized the NAACP's handling of a legal suit to ban *Birth of a Nation* and she often clashed with field representatives of the NAACP while she investigated lynchings. Wells-Barnett was also very critical of many of the NAACP's members, including Du Bois and Ovington. Wells-Barnett expressed admiration for Joel Spingarn, but she did not care for Du Bois. Wells-Barnett was also critical of Mary White Ovington. Wells-Barnett felt that Ovington's "heart is in this work," but Wells-Barnett pointed out that Ovington lacked the experience for such a job. Moreover, Wells-Barnett explained that Ovington "basked in the sunlight of the adoration of the few college-bred Negroes who have surrounded her, but has made little effort to know the soul of the black woman; and to that extent she has fallen far short of helping a race which has suffered as no white woman has ever been called upon to suffer or understand." Despite her differences with the NAACP, the NAACP would go on to become the leading organization in the anti-lynching crusade, while Wells-Barnett was becoming increasingly alienated and marginalized as a national leader.

Wells-Barnett was also an acquaintance of Marcus Garvey. During his time in Chicago, Garvey visited Mr. Barnett at his law office and Barnett subsequently brought Garvey home for dinner. During his conversation with the Barnetts, Garvey told them about the experience of black people in Jamaica and how they were dominated by the white minority there. Wells-Barnett pointed out that Garvey "made an impression on this country as no Negro before him had ever done." Despite this, she accused him of becoming "drunk with power" and in their private meetings together she expressed her doubts about Garvey's plans to launch the Black Star Line.

In 1918, the UNIA held a meeting, in which people were chosen to represent the UNIA at the Peace Conference in Versailles. Wells-Barnett and A. Philip Randolph were elected at this meeting to lobby on the behalf of the UNIA, although she never ended up going. Not long after this meeting, Wells-Barnett addressed a UNIA gathering in New York where she publicly advised against Garvey's plans to establish the Black Star Line. Garvey was not pleased by this. In the aftermath of the failures of Garvey's plans, Wells-Barnett had this to say: "Perhaps if Mr. Garvey had listened to my advice he need not have undergone the humiliations which afterward became his." What Wells-Barnett could not have known was that there was a serious attempt to undermine and destroy Garvey's plans. This included infiltrating the UNIA with spies and agents, and damaging some of the ships.

Wells-Barnett would later express regret for not taking a more active role in the NAACP, but there is no doubt that it was within the UNIA that Wells-Barnett could have an organization that would have appreciated her efforts and accommodated her views. Unlike Du Bois, Garvey genuinely admired Wells-Barnett's courage and wanted her to have an active role in his organization. In an article written for a Chicago magazine, Garvey included Wells-Barnett as being among the many great black leaders that he discovered in the United States. The UNIA was also an organization that preached and practiced economic empowerment for African people, as Wells-Barnett had advocated. Ultimately her apprehension of Garvey's schemes led Wells-Barnett to avoid embracing Garvey or the UNIA. Garvey's arrest and deportation seemed to have been confirmation to Wells-Barnett that her apprehensions were well-founded.

Not only did Wells-Barnett have difficulties working with other major leaders at the time, but she also had struggles organizing and maintaining her own organization. Following the Springfield riots, Wells-Barnett formed the Negro Fellowship League (NFL). The NFL established a settlement house in Chicago. The NFL was able to secure funding from Victor Lawson for the house, but when a black branch of the YMCA was opened in 1913, Lawson cut off his funding to the NFL and funded the YMCA instead.

In 1915, Eugene Kinckle Jones organized a branch of the Urban League in Chicago. Wells-Barnett saw the Urban League as a rival that "was brought to Chicago to supplant the activities of the Negro Fellowship League." To Wells-Barnett's disappointment, many of her friends joined this new group. Among them included Victor Lawson, who had previously withdrawn his funds to Wells-Barnett's organization. The Frederick Douglass Center, which

Wells-Barnett helped to found, provided rent-free use for the Urban League. Even the women's clubs that Wells-Barnett founded, which included a club that bore her name, gave their support to the Urban League. Further alienating Wells-Barnett was the fact that many key leaders in the Urban League were close friends of Booker T. Washington. By 1920, Wells-Barnett was forced to close the settlement house for good. By contrast, the Urban League was more effective than the NFL at providing employment for others. Linda McMurry pointed out that "Wells-Barnett contributed to her own loss of support through her temperament and actions. She tended to see other groups as competitors." McMurry also notes that Wells-Barnett's "confrontational approach and uncompromising self-righteousness disrupted most of the movements she joined."

Wells-Barnett also endured a number of challenges within the National Association of Colored Women (NACW). In 1899, the NACW met in Chicago and excluded Wells-Barnett from the meeting because some of the members refused to attend if Wells-Barnett was included. The fact that Washington had the support of the NACW would suggest that Wells-Barnett's conflicts with Washington led to her being alienated from the NACW. Wells-Barnett was never able to secure herself as a leader within the organization, and by 1924 she was defeated by Mary McLeod Bethune in the presidential election. Wells-Barnett's status in the NACW was such that when she attended a convention in 1909, she was hissed at by the other women. Wells-Barnett decided to go home rather than going to the banquet later that night.

Throughout her life, Wells-Barnett lacked any real massive support for any of her efforts. Wells-Barnett lost her job for criticizing the inferior education that black children received in Memphis schools. Wells-Barnett expected the support of black parents, but she did not receive that support. In 1930, Wells-Barnett ran as a candidate for the Senate, but she came in third place. She claimed: "Few women responded as I had hoped." These events and other disappointments demonstrated the difficulties that Wells-Barnett encountered in her fight for the rights of black people and it cannot be neglected that a lot of these disappointments were related to the fact that Wells-Barnett never had the backing of a national organization behind here in the way that many other leaders have had. We have already mentioned the organizational support that Washington, Du Bois, and Garvey had behind them, but we can look at later leaders such as Martin Luther King and Malcolm X who both had the support and backing of a larger organization or movement. Wells-Barnett, in the words of Thomas Holt, was a "lone warrior" waging a battle against racism. She did not have the benefit or support of a national organization.

Despite this, we cannot overlook the importance of Wells-Barnett's contribution to the struggle against racism, particularly her struggle against lynching. Through her campaigning and writing on the issue, Wells-Barnett was able to successfully expose the issue of lynching and bring it to the forefront. It was also her tactics that the NAACP employed in their own campaign against lynching. Wells-Barnett's views on self-defense were also the antecedent to activists such as Malcolm X, Kwame Ture, Robert F. Williams, Huey Newton, and others from the 1960s and 1970s that were vocal supporters of armed self-defense in the face of white aggression against black people.

Three years before her death Wells-Barnett wrote: "All at once the realization came to me that I had nothing to show for all those years of toil and labor." She was expressing the sum total of her years of disappointment and marginalization at the hands of her own people. Much of this was due to the fact that Wells-Barnett was never able to work with any of the major leaders throughout her lifetime or join any of the major organizations. Her criticisms of Booker T. Washington perhaps did the most to alienate her on a national stage, yet she had also refused to work with the NAACP after the slight she received from Du Bois. Similarly, Wells-Barnett also refused to work with the Urban League in Chicago and in turn the Urban League took with it much of Wells-Barnett's own supporters. Wells-Barnett refused to work with the UNIA because she was skeptical of Garvey, despite Garvey's own admiration for her. Isolated from working with the major national organizations of her time, Wells-Barnett's influence began to wane and she was becoming increasingly isolated even from the very clubs that she had founded. Perhaps the best testament to the neglect of Wells-Barnett was when Carter G. Woodson wrote a book on African American history. Wells-Barnett lamented that Woodson's book had neglected to mention her contributions.

References:

Ida B. Wells-Barnett, *Crusade for Justice: The Autobiography of Ida B. Wells* (Chicago: University of Chicago Press, 1970).

___ "Booker T. Washington and his Critics"

___ *Mob Rule in New Orleans*, 1900.

___ *Southern Horrors: Lynch Law in All Its Phases*, 1892.

Linda O. McMurry, *To Keep the Waters Troubled: The Life of Ida B. Wells,* (Oxford Press, 2000).

Louis R. Harlan, "Booker T. Washington and the White Man's Burden," The American Historical Review, Vol. 71, No. 2 (Jan., 1966), pp. 441-467

Thomas C. Holt, "The Lonely Warrior: Ida B. Wells-Barnett and the Struggle for Black Leaders," *Black Leaders of the Twentieth Century*, (University of Illinois Press, 1982), pp: 39-61

W.E.B. Du Bois, *The Souls of Black Folk*, 1903.

4

THE POLITICAL WEAKNESS OF THE PAN AFRICANIST CONGRESS

The Pan Africanist Congress (PAC) emerged out of the African National Congress (ANC) as a breakaway group led by elements within the ANC that had grown frustrated with the ANC's direction. Although the PAC's president, Robert Sobukwe, was one of the key anti-apartheid leaders, the PAC as a party failed to provide a real political alternative to the ANC. As will be demonstrated, the PAC had a number of issues which hindered their ability to challenge the ANC as the foremost organization in the struggle against apartheid.

The PAC was born in 1959 due to unsatisfied members within the ANC leaving for ideological reasons. There was a growing segment within the ANC that were referring to themselves as Africanists. When it became apparent the Africanists could not pursue their goals within the ANC, they split with the movement to form one of their own. There were some in the ANC such as Nthato Motlana who was sympathetic towards the beliefs of the Africanists, but also felt that the breakaway of the Africanists "led to a lot of strife." Outside of the ANC the Africanists, led by Sobukwe, were free to develop their ideology of African Nationalism.

Sobukwe argued that "the African people can be organised only under the banner of African nationalism in an All-African Organisation where they will by themselves formulate policies and programmes and decide on the methods of struggle without interference from either so-called left-wing or right-wing groups of the minorities who arrogantly appropriate to themselves the right to plan and think for the Africans." Sobukwe also maintained that the freedom of Africans in South Africa did not exclude the

119

Europeans or other people, but at the same time the PAC was also opposed to working with non-Africans. This seemed to cause a bit of confusion on where the PAC stood in terms of race because they argued that Asians and whites could be included as "Africans" if they accepted and embraced Africa as their homeland, yet Benjamin Pogrund pointed out that "the intention was certainly to restrict the possibility of non-Africans becoming members of the PAC." Sobukwe repeatedly expressed his belief in one human race, but the PAC was a party that excluded people on the basis of race. According to Pogrund, the PAC "believed intensely that it simply wasn't possible for people of other racial groups to share the struggle honestly with them." Further confusion was created when the PAC began accepting white and Indian members. In fact, Patrick Duncan had been the first white man accepted into the PAC. The PAC members that were imprisoned refused to believe that whites were being accepted into the PAC and claimed that this was nothing more than "ANC propaganda."

Sobukwe attempted to explain the exclusion of Europeans by explaining that whenever Europeans co-operated with African movements, they "kept demanding checks and counter-checks, guarantees and the like, with the result that they stultify and retard the movement of the Africans." He explained that the reason for this was that they were "protecting their sectional interests." He was also critical of the Indians for developing a "merchant class" which had become "tainted with the virus of national arrogance and cultural supremacy."

Pogrund points out that everyone was left dissatisfied because they felt that the Africanists had not justified their rejection of other groups. Pogrund further explains that Sobukwe and Mothopeng "were unable to fully validate the exclusion of all whites." The issue of coloreds (mixed race black people) also caused some confusion on where the PAC stood. Although Sobukwe said that the PAC would include coloreds, some within the PAC resented that coloreds "generally craved acceptance by whites and turned their backs on blacks." The PAC's position on race was further challenged when some pointed out that if the PAC would accept coloreds, why then not also accept the white parents of those coloreds.

The PAC put forward an agenda which sought to achieve freedom by 1963. This led Mandela to explain that the PAC "put forward a dramatic and overambitious program that promised quick solutions." This was indeed a very overambitious program, but one that the PAC felt it had to engage in nonetheless. Sobukwe explained "we are convinced that we shall be free by 1963, and towards that end we shall continue to struggle."

The PAC was initially greeted with support by some Afrikaner Nationalists that supported what they believed was an organization that promoted racial separatism. This changed when the Afrikaners realized that the PAC was struggling to overturn white domination in South Africa. The state began to take active steps to destabilize the PAC. To help weaken the Africanist movement, the Security Police attempted to foster division between the PAC and ANC through the use of fake leaflets. Sobukwe, recognizing such divisive tactics, stressed: "We have stated time and again that we are not fighting the ANC. Our battle is against white domination."

Despite the position on the ANC that was expressed by Sobukwe, Nelson Mandela recognized that certain elements in the PAC were competing with the ANC and described their relationship as "more competitive than cooperative." Zephania Mothopeng openly expressed his belief that the PAC was more "militant" and that the ANC should follow the PAC's lead. The PAC also refused to participate in meetings with the ANC. Mandela noted that the "PAC's insecurity occasionally had comical results." One example Mandela gives was when it was ordered that he should be isolated from other prisoners. PAC members in prison decided that Mothopeng should be isolated as well, so they had him work and eat separately from other prisoners. Mandela also found out that the PAC had been claiming that he left the ANC and had joined them. Pogrund heard these rumors as well and when he asked Sobukwe about it, Sobukwe responded that the rumors were not true.

An even more obvious example of how the PAC was actively working against the ANC was when Mandela went to Ethiopia.

Mandela and Oliver Tambo attended a meeting there, only to find that their application for accreditation was blocked by a delegate from Uganda because the delegate felt that the ANC was a tribal organization for Xhosas. Their application was accepted once they proved that the ANC was in fact not a tribal organization, but the whole ordeal made Mandela aware of the fact that many Africans only knew about the ANC from the false depiction that the PAC had spread about them.

The PAC had also spread reports that the Umkhonto we Sizwe was the "brainchild of the Communist Party and the Liberal Party," which was not true and in fact both parties had been on bad terms with each other. Even more damning was the claim that the ANC was using Africans as "cannon fodder." Mandela described the actions of the PAC as a "blatant case of opportunism." He also noted that the PAC's actions were motivated more by a desire to eclipse the ANC than to defeat the enemy. To highlight this, Mandela explains how the PAC had opposed the ANC's anti-pass campaign:

> The PAC at the time appeared lost; they were a leadership in search of followers, and they had yet to initiate any action that put them on the political map. They knew of the ANC's antipass campaign and had been invited to join, but instead of linking arms with the Congress movement, they sought to sabotage us.

The PAC went ahead and launched its own anti-pass campaign shortly before the ANC did. Sobukwe invited the ANC to join the demonstration four days before it was to take place, but the ANC declined to participate, however. Mandela felt that it was a tactical move that was meant to shield the PAC from criticisms of excluding the ANC. For the PAC the pass campaign was an important step towards achieving the freedom that they promised by 1963 and for Sobukwe it was very important that the leadership of the PAC be on the frontlines of this campaign. Sobukwe was a strong believer in leadership making the same sacrifices as the masses. He wrote: "When we embark on a campaign it will be the leaders who will be in front. They will not remain behind while the

122

masses rot in gaol."

The PAC launched their anti-pass campaign on March 21, 1960. Sobukwe and his followers marched to the police station to turn themselves in. Sobukwe told the officers: "I am Sobukwe. We have no passes and we want the police to arrest us." This apparently confused the police officers, who did not arrest the PAC members initially. In other locations, the police responded with violence. In a place called Bophelong, the police had opened fire and killed two people. In Sharpeville, where thousands of unarmed black people had organized, the police opened fire on the demonstrators, killing about sixty-nine of them and injuring over 180 others.

One journalist reported that when Sobukwe heard of the massacre at Sharpeville he was depressed and "almost to the point of tears [...]." As a result of the anti-pass campaign by the PAC, Sobukwe, Mothopeng, and leaders within the PAC were arrested. Others were sent out of the country to avoid arrest. This would turn out to be one of the greatest mistakes made by the PAC, as Pogrund explained:

> Faulty planning by the PAC was now evident because, with almost all the leadership either in jail or sent out of the country, there was no certainty about the chain of command.

Although the ANC did not join the PAC in their anti-pass campaign, the ANC used the PAC's campaign to their advantage. According to Mandela, the PAC's campaign forced the ANC to "make rapid adjustments" to the new situation. In response to the events that transpired during the PAC's anti-pass campaign and the Sharpeville massacre, Chief Luthuli burned his pass and called on others to do the same. Luthuli also announced a national Day of Mourning for the massacre at Sharpeville. Mandela and Duma Nokwe joined Luthuli by burning their passes in front of hundreds of people.

While in prison, Sobukwe criticized the ANC's actions. He accused them of "opportunism" and criticized them for launching a national day of mourning for the Sharpeville massacre on March 28, rather than their previously planned pass demonstrations. Sobukwe further complained that the ANC opposed the PAC's anti-pass campaign, dismissing it as "sensational, ill-defined and ill-planned." Sobukwe continued:

> The ANC is now trying to bask in the sunshine of PAC's successes. Luthuli now has the courage which he has lacked for over twelve years to burn his reference book after passes had been suspended. Supported and boosted by the white Press, he has been making one foolish statement after the other, pretending that he has a following in the country.

Sobukwe then warned the ANC: "Hands off our campaign. We don't need your interference. Go on with your coffin carrying and other childish pastimes but leave the African people to fight their struggle without you." These were strong words from Sobukwe that spoke to the mistrust between the ANC and PAC at the time. Pogrund argued that Sobukwe had "misjudged" the "mood of huge numbers of black people, including those in PAC strongholds." Thousands of Africans across the nation heeded Luthuli's call for mourning. Sobukwe criticized the ANC for their opportunism in attempting to co-opt the PAC's campaign, but with the PAC's key leaders in prison or outside the country, it was left to the ANC to respond in the aftermath of the Sharpeville massacre.

The activities of the PAC and ANC in the aftermath of the Sharpeville massacre clearly worried the government in South Africa. The government responded by outlawing both the ANC and PAC, and declaring a state of emergency. It was around this time that Mandela was arrested. He was awoken in the middle of the night and taken away from his home.

In prison Mandela communicated with Sobukwe. The two genuinely respected each other and were good friends, although they differed on some issues. For instance, Mandela felt that the prisoners should fight for better living conditions, whereas

124

Sobukwe held the view that doing so acknowledged that the government had a right to detain them as prisoners in the first place. Mandela was also critical of the PAC's slogan "Freedom in 1963." Mandela felt that it was wrong for an organization to give people false hope by making promises it could not keep. Indeed, freedom would not come in 1963 or in Sobukwe's lifetime for that matter.

The issue of violent resistance against the apartheid regime is an interesting one that seemed to have created divisions both within the ANC and the PAC. Both parties initially began fighting the apartheid system by using non-violent methods, but the increasing violence of the apartheid regime made continuing such non-violent methods rather difficult. Mandela explained, "Africans had either to accept inferiority or fight against it by violence. We chose the latter." Sobukwe was a strong believer in non-violence. Mothopeng explained that Sobukwe was "too much of a Christian" to renounce the concept of non-violence, yet Sobukwe seemed to have come to accept that "the ruled could not avoid turning to violence." Despite Sobukwe's reservations about violence, elements in the PAC turned towards extreme violence to achieve their goals.

The armed wing of the PAC was Poqo. There was doubt among some in the PAC that Sobukwe actually knew about Poqo, despite the fact that court trials mentioned Sobukwe in connection with Poqo. Zolile Hamilton Keke stated: "Had Sobukwe known of it he would have vetoed it," because Sobukwe would not have approved of a situation in which "people with pangas and stones were given orders to attack well trained Boers." The reality was that Sobukwe's imprisonment made it difficult for him to be involved in key decisions within the party and this allowed Poqo to form without Sobukwe's direction or input. Pogrund stated that "by the time Poqo developed there is no indication that Sobukwe was still in control of the PAC."

Z.B. Molete explained that "Leballo always claimed Poqo as the PAC's military wing but it wasn't formed by the PAC." Despite this, many members of the PAC did view Poqo as an extension of the organization. Unlike the Umkhonto we Sizwe of the ANC, Poqo's actions were less organized and coordinated. Poqo's main objective seemed to have been simply to kill as many white people as they could. To this effect they produced a slogan; "One settler, one bullet." The creation of Poqo was just one of the many indicators of the unorganized nature of the PAC at the time. According to Pogrund, Sobukwe's imprisonment "provided the opportunity for angry young men to make the running, and for Leballo to move in and to steer them as his own, as his means of asserting leadership."

While in prison Sobukwe closely monitored American politics. Sobukwe greatly admired President Lyndon Johnson. He wrote that Johnson was "the hope of all who stand for non-racialism." Sobukwe also wrote of Johnson: "I like Johnson. I don't think he is devious. I don't think he is very complex either. He isn't an intellectual, but then there are very few in the political field. His touch is very deft in domestic matters [...] He has one outstanding virtue for which I like him." Sobukwe was uncritical of Johnson's policy concerning Vietnam. He felt that America was "not in Vietnam for any imperialist purposes." Sobukwe also believed that if American troops withdrew from Vietnam, "Cambodia, Thailand, and the rest of the Archipelago would face communist bids for power."

Sobukwe was disappointed to hear that Johnson had withdrawn as a candidate for the 1969 elections. Sobukwe was not so supportive of Robert Kennedy's bid for the presidency. He wrote that he was "rather disgusted" with Kennedy and described his behavior as "ruthless opportunism." Sobukwe explained that he could forgive "Johnson's blunders" but he could not support Kennedy. When Kennedy was assassinated shortly after, Sobukwe was disappointed. He wrote: "I did not want him dead. I wanted him to be beaten by McCarthy. Failure would have done him a lot of good."

Sobukwe's support of Johnson is interesting given the rapidly declining public opinion of Johnson in the United States. Sobukwe's admiration of Johnson reflected a certain naiveté that Sobukwe had in political matters in that personally liking someone was enough for Sobukwe. Pogrund was a bit frustrated by this when Sobukwe had insisted that he liked Minister P.C. Pelser, the same man who re-enacted the Sobukwe Clause, which extended Sobukwe's time in prison. Sobukwe, who had met with Pelser in person, insisted that he liked Pelser and even defended Pelser's decision to keep him jailed. The whole exchange about Pelser left Pogrund to wonder if Sobukwe's tolerance was a strength or weakness. Such tolerance certainly led Sobukwe to misjudge certain personalities both in the United States and in South Africa.

Sobukwe studied other political issues, including Israel's victory in the 1967 war. While musing over the events that took place, Sobukwe concluded that it would be in Israel's best interest to seek some form of peace with the Arabs to avoid further conflicts. Sobukwe cited South Africa's own history as a model to follow from:

> Moshoeshoe 1 (nineteenth-century King of Basuto), when attacked by the Zulus, inflicted a crushing defeat on them at Thaba Bosiu and, as they retreated, sent a large herd of cattle to "his brothers". The Zulus never again attacked him.

Sobukwe also expressed apprehension over whether the Arabs living in North Africa were African or Arab. Sobukwe felt that if they viewed themselves as Africans then they should not have been so involved in the affairs of the Middle East. Sobukwe also examined whether or not Afro-Americans and West Indians could be Pan-Africanists, to which Sobukwe concluded that he would not include them in his definition of Pan-Africanism. This was an interesting consideration given that Sobukwe had previously mentioned the oppression of African Americans and West Indians when speaking on the global oppression of African people. In this same speech Sobukwe also quoted the Jamaican born Pan-Africanist Marcus Garvey. Mothopeng took a different position, however. According to Pogrund, Mothopeng had made a speech where he called for all black people to return to Africa.

Although Sobukwe seemed to have excluded Afro-Americans from his definition of Pan-Africanism, there were a number of blacks in the United States that had a growing interest in South Africa. The National Association for the Advancement of Colored People (NAACP) had offered Sobukwe a job. Congressman Andrew Young and tennis star Arthur Ashe both visited Kimberly in 1974 and met with Sobukwe. Young had much to praise about Sobukwe after spending two hours with him. Young said that Sobukwe is "a real leader of the African people." Young offered to take Sobukwe's two oldest children to his home in Atlanta to ensure that they were given better schooling. Sobukwe was eager to have his children go to the United States and agreed to this. Despite the apprehensions that the government in South Africa had about letting black students study abroad, Sobukwe's children Miliswa and Dini went to live with Young in the United States.

A year later Ashe made another trip to South Africa, but this time he did not visit Sobukwe, despite telling Pogrund that he had planned to. Andrew Young also returned to South Africa. According to Pogrund, Young arrived "in a blaze of publicity and friends." Young was no longer a congressman. He was an ambassador who arrived in South Africa on the invitation of Harry Oppenheimer. Young did not contact Sobukwe at all and being ignored by Young greatly hurt Sobukwe.

Despite being isolated in Kimberly, Sobukwe was firm in his belief that he could still play a relevant role in politics. The PAC was certainly in desperate need of Sobukwe's leadership, as the party had not recovered from the jailing of its leadership in 1960. At the time Leballo was serving as the president in exile in Tanzania and the PAC had essentially been rendered ineffective in South Africa. Despite this, the African Nationalist ideas of the PAC would influence the Black Consciousness Movement led by Steve Biko.

Much as Sobukwe had done, Biko challenged the role of white liberals in the black struggle. Biko held Sobukwe in high regard and it was obvious that Biko was heavily influenced by many of Sobukwe's ideas. In one instance Biko walked into a room where Sobukwe was. Biko held Sobukwe in such high regard that he exclaimed: "What! Even God is here!" Despite Biko's reverence for Sobukwe, there was also disagreement between the two over some of Biko's private conduct. Sobukwe seemed to have some concern over the behaviors of Biko and others around him. Father Aelred Stubbs, a white priest who was close with Biko and other members of the South African Students' Organisation (SASO) expressed his concern to Sobukwe over their behavior. Stubbs was concerned over the "heavy drinking and excessive womanising" on the part of the students. Sobukwe did not approve of this behavior either. When Stubbs voiced Sobukwe's concerns to the leaders of SASO, Barney Pityana was supportive, but Stubbs noted that Biko "reacted vigorously."

Despite the ban placed on Sobukwe, leaders of the BCM met with him regularly, doing so in secret. When Sobukwe's mother died, Sobukwe was given permission to return to his birthplace and had to report to the police once arriving and leaving. On his way back to Kimberley, Sobukwe stopped to meet with Biko, even though Biko had also been banned at this point. Afterwards, the two kept in touch.

By 1977, Sobukwe was seriously ill. Some believed that there might have been a conspiracy involved, although Sobukwe's poor health should be no surprise given that Sobukwe was a smoker. Sobukwe himself suggested to Mothopeng that he had been poisoned while he was in prison. Despite his illness, Sobukwe remained upbeat. Pogrund recalled that when he went to give Sobukwe comfort "it was not I that gave him comfort, but it was he who gave me comfort." Being relegated to Kimberley prevented Sobukwe from getting the specialized medical attention that he needed. Sobukwe died in February 1978.

The PAC had never recovered from Sobukwe's jailing in 1960. One of the things that made Sobukwe's death such a devastating blow for the PAC is because the PAC did not have another leader of Sobukwe's caliber. Without solid leadership, the PAC was in confusion and disarray. The party was further plagued with internal disputes. By contrast, the ANC had maintained its stability despite the attempts made by the apartheid regime to suppress the party.

Even with many of its key leaders such as Mandela in prison, the ANC still managed to maintain a strong and coherent political presence.

Mothopeng was elected president of the PAC in 1986. Two years later he was released from prison. In 1990, the PAC rejected the talks that were being held with the government of South Africa. This too showed confusion and inconsistency on the part of the PAC. The PAC rejected the negotiations with the government, but those talks eventually led to South Africa's first nonracial election in 1994. The PAC argued internally about whether or not to participate in the election. Mandela explained that the "PAC feared democratic elections because they knew such a vote would expose their meager popular support." This proved to be true, as the PAC finally decided to participate in the election in 1994, but only won one percent of the total votes. Much of this had to do with the fact that the PAC never laid out clear political objectives, beyond calling for a return of the land.

Ultimately, the PAC was never able to establish itself as a clear alternative to the ANC. This was due to a wide number of factors. Sobukwe's jailing essentially cut him off from the rest of the organization, leaving the PAC without its leader. Moreover, the PAC degenerated into rivalries and divisions among leaders with their own goals and agendas. Although Sobukwe himself did not appear to have any serious animosity towards the ANC, there were members of the PAC that were actively competing with and working against the ANC, which further weakened their position in the national struggle. The PAC also suffered from ideological issues. It was pointed out before that their position on the question of race left many confused and unsatisfied. The PAC also never had a clear policy concerning violent resistance, resulting in a much less organized and coordinated military effort than what the ANC had conducted. By the time negotiations were being held in 1990, the PAC not only lacked popular political support but they also did not have a consistent position regarding whether or not they would join in the negotiations.

References:

Benjamin Pogrund, *How Can Man Die Better*, 1997.

Nelson Mandela, *Long Walk to Freedom*, 1995.

5

HERITAGE OR HATE

On June 17, 2015, a 21 year old white supremacist named Dylann Roof opened fire at the Emanuel African Methodist Episcopal Church in Charleston, South Carolina, during a Bible study. The shooting resulted in the deaths of nine people: Cynthia Hurd, Susie Jackson, Ethel Lee Lance, Depayne Middleton-Doctor, Tywanza Sanders, Daniel Simmons, Myra Thompson, Sharonda Coleman Singleton, and Senator Clementa Pinckney.

The shooting sparked a national debate around the rest of the country about the place of the Confederate flag in American society. For some the flag was a symbol of racial hatred and slavery. Others argued that the flag was merely a symbol of Southern heritage and pride. The reality of the debate is that there is truth in both sides. In the aftermath of the shooting at Charlestown, President Barack Obama gave a eulogy for Reverend Clementa Pinckney. One of the most important things that Obama mentioned in his speech was the conflicting opinions on the Confederate flag:

> For too long, we were blind to the pain that the Confederate flag stirred in too many of our citizens. It's true, a flag did not cause these murders. But as people from all walks of life, Republicans and Democrats, now acknowledge—including Governor Haley, whose recent eloquence on the subject is worthy of praise—as we all have to acknowledge, the flag has always represented more than just ancestral pride.

Some view the flag as a testament to the courage and bravery of those who fought and died for the Confederacy. For some the flag is even a symbol of liberty and resistance against the tyranny of the North. Dubbed by some to be the "War of Northern Aggression," the Confederacy is depicted as a confederacy of states that were defending their rights from the forceful impositions of the North. For this reason such people have argued that the war was not fought over slavery, but that it was fought over the issue of state's rights. As I will get to, slavery was in fact a central issue in the war. It was the slavery in Confederate states that motivated many black people to fight on the side of the North.

I will not get into the notion of the "War of Northern Aggression" or the idea that the South was unfairly victimized by the North solely because after the Compromise of 1877 when federal troops were withdrawn from the South, it was truthfully black people who suffered the most in the aftermath of the Civil War, not white Southerners.

From a national perspective one can appreciate why the flag is divisive. It represents a period in American history when America was literally at war with itself, and as a result it was the bloodiest war in American history. In the aftermath of the war, President Abraham Lincoln was assassinated by a Confederate sympathizer, making him the first president in the history of the United States to be assassinated. For these reasons it is difficult to see the Confederate flag as a symbol of pride because of the negative history that is associated with the flag.

Although one cannot deny that the South fought valiantly, they still lost the war. That loss was a victory for the United States and a victory for enslaved Africans who were now given their emancipation. So we may ask what pride does one demonstrate by displaying the flag of the Confederacy? The Confederacy committed an act of treason, lost the war that followed, and America as a nation was made better because of it. This is why it is a bit ironic that those who claim to be patriotic Americans would wave a flag that represents the division of America. Had the Confederacy won, the South would have been a separate political entity from the North and thus there would be no "United" States of America as such.

Moreover, it was no accident that Dylann Roof used the

Confederate flag as a symbol to bolster his ideology. He saw that flag in the same light as the apartheid South African and the Rhodesian flags—that is, as flags that represent white supremacy and white domination over black people because that is what the founders of all three political entities had envisioned. The place of the Confederate flag in Southern (and in American) history cannot be ignored, but that should not be confused with seeing the flag as a celebration of Southern pride and heritage. This is especially true of black people who uphold the Confederate flag thinking that the flag represents heritage, yet fail to even understand their own heritage and history as a people who have struggled against both the Confederate and American flags for their liberation.

The most debated aspect of the Confederate flag is regarding the issue of race. I will say from the beginning that the flag itself is not necessarily a symbol of racism. That is to say that many people who proudly display the flag are not necessarily themselves racists, but one must also understand the ideology of racial supremacy which underpinned the Confederacy. This is precisely why some abolitionists, such as Martin Delany, came to oppose the Confederacy.

Leading up to the Civil War, Delany was working on establishing a settlement in Africa for black people to migrate to. He believed that for black people to achieve their freedom they had to leave the United States, but with the outbreak of the Civil War, Delany changed his plans. Delany believed that the Civil War was a war against slavery and for this reason he recruited black men to fight for the Union. Delany was given the opportunity to hold an interview with President Abraham Lincoln, which resulted in Delany being named the first black field officer in American history.

The abolitionist Harriet Tubman, who used to sneak onto slave plantations and help slaves to escape to freedom, was also motivated to fight against the Confederacy due to the issue of slavery. She worked as a spy for the Union army during the war. During the war Tubman led a raid on Combahee River, which led to the liberation of over 700 slaves.

The abolitionist Frederick Douglass advocated for black soldiers to be recruited to fight for the Union. Like Tubman and

Delany, Douglass saw a Union victory in the war as the key to ending slavery for good. Henry Highland Garnet, an abolitionist and proponent of emigration to Africa like Delany, was also a supporter of the Union side of the war. Sojourner Truth was yet another black abolitionist that supported the Union cause in the war. It is no coincidence that many of those who fought for black freedom prior to the war supported the Union during the war.

One could argue that there were black people that served the Confederacy so the Civil War was not fought along racial lines, but this leads one to ask which black abolitionist supported the Confederate cause? In fact, many of the blacks that served the Confederacy during the war were slaves that were merely doing the bidding of their masters. Therefore, if we take the position that the Confederate flag is not about racism, we still cannot ignore the reality that during the Civil War black freedom fighters supported the Union side of the war because they believed that in defeating the Confederacy they would achieve the liberation of black people. History has demonstrated that they were correct in this view.

Ignoring these facts does not change the realities of the Civil War or the Confederacy. We can take this even further and look at the opinion of the Confederate states themselves. The *Charleston Mercury*, a newspaper in South Carolina, ran a story which stated:

> In 1860 South Carolina seceded alone from the old union of States. Her people, in Convention assembled, invited the slaveholding States (none others) of the old Union to join her in erecting a separate Government of Slave States, for the protection of their common interests. All of the slave states, with the exception of Maryland and Kentucky, responded to her invitation. The Southern Confederacy of slave States was formed.
>
> It was on account of encroachments upon the institution of slavery by the sectional majority of the old Union, that South Carolina seceded from that Union. It is not at this late day, after the loss of thirty thousand of her best and bravest men in

battle, that she will suffer it to be bartered away; or ground between the upper and nether mill stones, by the madness of Congress, or the counsels of shallow men elsewhere.

By the compact we made with Virginia and the other States of this Confederacy, South Carolina will stand to the bitter end of destruction. By that compact she intends to stand or to fall. Neither Congress, nor certain makeshift men in Virginia, can force upon her their mad schemes of weakness and surrender. She stands upon her institutions—and there she will fall in their defence. We want no Confederate Government without our institutions. And we will have none. Sink or swim, live or die, we stand by them, and are fighting for them this day. That is the ground of our fight—it is well that all should understand it at once. Thousands and tens of thousands of the bravest men, and the best blood of this State, fighting in the ranks, have left their bones whitening on the bleak hills of Virginia in this cause. We are fighting for our system of civilization—not for buncomb, or for Jeff Davis. We intend to fight for that, or nothing. We expect Virginia to stand beside us in that fight, as of old, as we have stood beside her in this war up to this time. But such talk coming from such a source is destructive to the cause. Let it cease at once, in God's name, and in behalf of our common cause! It is [paralyzing] to every man here to hear it. It throws a pall over the hearts of the soldiers from this State to hear it. The soldiers of South Carolina will not fight beside a nigger'to talk of emancipation is to disband our army. We are free men, and we chose to fight for ourselves—we want no slaves to fight for us…. Hack at the root of the Confederacy—our institutions—our civilization—and you kill the cause as dead as a boiled crab.

As the above passage indicates, South Carolina seceded over the issue of slavery. Defenders of the Confederacy may argue that slavery was not the case of the war, but the Confederate states themselves made it clear that they were fighting in defense of the institution of slavery. George Williamson, the secession commissioner of Louisiana, explained:

The people of Louisiana were unwilling to endanger their liberties and property by submission to the despotism of a single tyrant, or the canting tyranny of pharisaical majorities. Insulted by the denial of her constitutional equality by the non-slaveholding States, outraged by their contemptuous rejection of proffered compromises, and convinced that she was illustrating the capacity of her people for self-government by withdrawing from a union that had failed, without fault of hers, to accomplish its purposes, she declared herself a free and independent State on the 26th day of January last. History affords no example of a people who changed their government for more just or substantial reasons. Louisiana looks to the formation of a Southern confederacy to preserve the blessings of African slavery, and of the free institutions of the founders of the Federal Union, bequeathed to their posterity. As her neighbor and sister State, she desires the hearty co-operation of Texas in the formation of a Southern Confederacy. She congratulates herself on the recent disposition evinced by your body to meet this wish, by the election of delegates to the Montgomery convention. Louisiana and Texas have the same language, laws and institutions. Between the citizens of each exists the most cordial social and commercial intercourse. The Red river and the Sabine form common highways for the transportation of their produce to the markets of the world. Texas affords to the commerce of Louisiana a large portion of her products, and in exchange the banks of New Orleans furnish Texas with her only paper circulating medium. Louisiana supplies to Texas a market for her surplus wheat, grain and stock; both States have large areas of fertile, uncultivated lands, peculiarly adapted to slave labor; and they are both so deeply interested in African slavery that it may be said to be absolutely necessary to their existence, and is the

137

keystone to the arch of their prosperity. Each of the States has an extended Gulf coast, and must look with equal solicitude to its protection now, and the acquisition of the entire control of the Gulf of Mexico in due time. No two States of this confederacy are so identified in interest, and whose destinies are so closely interwoven with each other. Nature, sympathy and unity of interest make them almost one. Recognizing these facts, but still confident in her own powers to maintain a separate existence, Louisiana regards with great concern the vote of the people of Texas on the ratification of the ordinance of secession, adopted by your honorable body on the 1st of the present month. She is confident a people who so nobly and gallantly achieved their liberties under such unparalleled difficulties will not falter in maintaining them now. The Mexican yoke could not have been more galling to "the army of heroes" of '36 than the Black republican rule would be to the survivors and sons of that army at the present day.

The people of Louisiana would consider it a most fatal blow to African slavery, if Texas either did not secede or having seceded should not join her destinies to theirs in a Southern Confederacy. If she remains in the union the abolitionists would continue their work of incendiarism and murder. Emigrant aid societies would arm with Sharp's rifles predatory bands to infest her northern borders. The Federal Government would mock at her calamity in accepting the recent bribes in the army bill and Pacific railroad bill, and with abolition treachery would leave her unprotected frontier to the murderous inroads of hostile savages. Experience justifies these expectations. A professedly friendly federal administration gave Texas no substantial protection against the Indians or abolitionists, and what must she look for from an administration avowedly inimical and supported by no vote within her borders. Promises won from the timid and faithless are poor hostages of good faith. As a separate republic, Louisiana remembers too well the whisperings of European diplomacy for the abolition of slavery in the times of annexation not to be apprehensive of bolder demonstrations from the same quarter and the North in this country. The people of the slaveholding States are bound together by the same necessity and determination to preserve African slavery. The isolation of any one of them from the others would make her a theatre for abolition emissaries from the North and from Europe. Her existence would be one of constant peril to herself and of imminent danger to other neighboring slave-holding communities. A decent respect for the opinions and interests of the Gulf States seems to indicate that Texas should co-operate with them. I am authorized to say to your honorable body that Louisiana does not expect any beneficial result from the peace conference now assembled at Washington. She is unwilling that her action should depend on the border States. Her interests are identical with Texas and the seceding States. With them she will at present co-operate, hoping and believing in his own good time God will awaken the people of the border States to the vanity of asking for, or depending upon, guarantees or compromises wrung from a people whose consciences are too sublimated to be bound by that sacred compact, the constitution of the late United States. That constitution the Southern States have never violated, and taking it as the basis of our new government we hope to form a slave-holding confederacy that will secure to us and our remotest posterity the great blessings its authors designed in the Federal Union. With the social balance wheel of slavery to regulate its machinery, we may fondly indulge the hope that our Southern government will be perpetual.

There are other statements which demonstrate the centrality of slavery to the ideology and beliefs of Confederate states. In its declaration of "Immediate Causes which Induce and Justify the Secession of the State of Mississippi from the Federal Union," Mississippi explained:

> Our position is thoroughly identified with the institution of slavery—the greatest material interest of the world. Its labor supplies the product which constitutes by far the largest and most important portions of commerce of the earth. These products are peculiar to the climate verging on the tropical regions, and by an imperious law of nature, none but the black race can bear exposure to the tropical sun. These products have become necessities of the world, and a blow at slavery is a blow at commerce and civilization. That blow has been long aimed at the institution, and was at the point of reaching its consummation.

Some argue that the Civil War was not fought over the issue of slavery, but slavery was in fact a central issue to the war on both sides. Again, I do not argue that one is necessarily a racist for proudly displaying the Confederate flag, but on some level one must also recognize the historical realities of the Confederate flag. No black person during the Civil War who was serious about black freedom and about abolishing slavery would have fought for that flag or endorsed it. This is why it is especially puzzling to find black people who defend the Confederate flag. They may have the freedom to do so, but they enjoy their freedoms only because of the men and women that fought in opposition to the Confederacy.

Finally, it should be pointed out that Dylann Roof, an unapologetic white supremacist, saw the Confederate flag as a symbol of white supremacy and black suppression. Roof was also fond of the Rhodesian and apartheid South African flags as well for the same reasons. The thing that all three flags have in common is that they represent political entities in which the black population lived under the oppression of the white population. One may argue that the Confederate flag was not about racism or hate, but one also cannot ignore the fact that Roof's personal beliefs on race are very similar to those of the slave owning secessionists of the Confederacy.

As critical as I have been of the South, I do not want to give one the impression that the North was completely innocent either. Although leading up to the Civil War slavery had been abolished in the Northern states, Walter Rodney argued that Northern states merely moved away from slavery because they had found a more productive economic system:

> Slavery is useful for early accumulation of capital, but it is too rigid for industrial development. Slaves had to be given crude non-breakable tools which held back the capitalist development of agriculture and industry. That explains the fact that the northern portions of the U.S.A. gained far more industrial benefits from slavery than the South which actually had slave institutions on its soil; and ultimately the stage was reached during the American Civil War when the Northern capitalists fought to end slavery within the boundaries of the U.S.A., so that the country as a whole could advance to a higher level of capitalism.

As Rodney pointed out, after industrialization in the North slave labor was no longer as effective as factory labor, so the shift away from slavery and towards industrial labor was one done largely due to financial considerations. Moreover, the slave trade itself was dominated by Northern states, so although the North eventually came to abolish slavery, it only did so after it had already profited from slave labor and from the slave trade. At the time of the Civil War, the South was not as technologically advanced and was still reliant on slave labor.

The end of slavery did not result in the end of racism or black exploitation in either the North or the South. Malcolm X once accurately said as long as you are south of the Canadian border, you are in the South. This was because as far as the Union side of the war was concerned, it was a war to preserve the union. It was not a war fought to guarantee equal rights to African people. For

President Abraham Lincoln, who is often praised as being a great emancipator, the primary concern was holding together the Union. He wrote to Horace Greeley, explaining:

> My paramount object in this struggle is to save the Union, and is not either to save or to destroy slavery. If I could save the Union without freeing any slave I would do it, and if I could save it by freeing all the slaves I would do it; and if I could save it by freeing some and leaving others alone I would also do that. What I do about slavery, and the colored race, I do because I believe it helps to save the Union; and what I forbear, I forbear because I do not believe it would help to save the Union.

C.L.R. James writes: "It was the pressure of war which forced him to accept emancipation." It was also the pressure of the war that forced Lincoln to begin enlisting black soldiers to support the war effort. Even within the Union army there was racism. Delany had raised the issue of the poor treatment that black people experienced in the Union army. In his meeting with Lincoln, Delany complained about "the heartless and almost relentless prejudice exhibited towards the blacks by the Union army," and proposed "an army of blacks, commanded entirely by black officers" as a solution. Delany argued that "there exists too much prejudice among the whites for the soldiers to serve under a black commander, or the officers to be willing to associate with him."

The point to be made here is that Lincoln did not go into the Civil War with the intentions of establishing racial equality or abolishing slavery. Abolishing slavery for Lincoln was a side issue to the larger issue of holding together the Union. Since his assassination in 1865, Lincoln has been remembered as a great emancipator of black people, but there were greater political issues at play that motivated Lincoln to issue the "Emancipation Proclamation" in 1863. In fact, that proclamation only declared the freedom of slaves that were in Confederate states, but the proclamation did not include the Border States that were slave states which had not seceded from the Union. Slavery would finally be abolished completely in 1865 with the passage of the

Thirteenth Amendment.

An example of just how racist the North could be was the case of a Congolese man named Ota Benga, who was featured at a zoo in New York. Ota's family was killed by the Force Publique in the Congo while he was away on a hunt. Although Ota escaped the attack on his village that killed his family, he was captured and taken as a slave. Ota was later bought by an American and taken to the Louisiana Purchase Exposition as a display in 1904. From here, Ota was eventually taken to the Bronx Zoo in New York in 1906 where he was once again placed on display. Ota desired to return back home and gradually became depressed. Realizing that he would never return to his homeland, Ota committed suicide on March 29, 1916. Ota was used as an example of the inferiority of black people. In response to the criticisms of having Ota displayed at the zoo, *The New York Times* declared: "It is absurd to make moan over the imagined humiliation and degradation Benga is suffering."

In pointing out the racism of the Confederate states it is also important to point out that the North was just as racist, so the Civil War was not a war between a "good side" and a "bad side" as some may think of it. As far as African people were concerned, both sides were bad sides and they made this view very well-known. Yet they understood that a Union victory would advance the cause of African liberation in the United States, so they served the Union cause.

The history of the Civil War is often seen from the perspective of either the Union States or the Confederate states, but there is little consideration of the African role in the war. Some of the black people that fought for the Union did not do so out of a blind sense of patriotism. Prior to the war Martin Delany was an advocate of migration to Africa and would once again take up this position in the aftermath of the Reconstruction Era. Harriet Tubman led runaway slaves to Canada where they could live freely. The profound racism in the United States led both of them to advocate migration out of the United States at various points of their lives. Lincoln was concerned about holding together the Union, but for those like Delany and Tubman the Union had long since failed African people and their primary concern was the abolition of slavery and the liberation of their people.

In conclusion we return to the issue of whether or not the Confederate flag represents heritage or hate. Those who see the flag as being a proud part of their heritage certainly may never be convinced otherwise, but the reality is that during the Civil War that flag represented oppression and slavery so far as black people were concerned and it was those same people who rose up and fought against the Confederacy to achieve their liberation.

Selected References:

Abraham Lincoln, "Letter to Horace Greeley," August 22, 1862.

C.L.R. James, *A History of Pan-African Revolt*, (PM Press, 2012).

"Declaration of Causes of the Seceding States-Mississippi," 1861.

Frank A. Rollin, *Life and Public Services of Martin R. Delany*

George Williamson, "Address of George Williamson, Commissioner from Louisiana to the Texas Secession Convention," February 11, 1861.

Mitch Keller, "The Scandal at the Zoo," *New York Times*, August 6, 2006.

"We Want No Confederacy without Slavery," *Charleston Mercury*, 1865.

6

A CRITICAL ASSESSMENT OF MUHAMMAD ALI AS A POLITICAL FIGURE

Some of the most famous and wealthy African Americans in the United States have been athletes. Men such as Muhammad Ali, Michael Jordan, Tiger Woods, Kobe Bryant, and LeBron James have all become international icons. Yet, one is struck by the fact that in an era with so many successful black athletes, African Americans as a whole have continued to struggle. This was something that the Guyanese scholar and activist Walter Rodney was keen to point out in his book *The Groundings with My Brothers*:

> Many blacks live in that supposedly great society at a level of existence comparable to blacks in the poorest section of the colonial world. The blacks in the U.S. have no power. They have achieved prominence in a number of ways—they can sing, they can run, they can box, play baseball, etc., but they have no power.

What Rodney explains here is that even when black people succeed in certain fields, such as sports, that success does not translate into real empowerment. To understand why this is one must understand the historical development of the African athlete on the slave plantations. The African athlete was essentially an entertainer on the slave plantation, who was used to sometimes to earn money for his master.

I wish to begin this assessment by discussing the historical role of the African athlete, which traces its origins back to the slave plantations. There is a novel called *Mandingo* about Mede, a slave who would fight other slaves in competitions that the slave masters

145

would bet on. Mede's story has a historical counterpart in that of Tom Molineaux, who used to box other slaves on the plantation for the entertainment of the slave masters. His master was able to earn much money from betting on Molineaux. Molineaux was eventually able to earn his freedom. He made his living as a boxer in Europe, but eventually died in poverty at the age of 34. The story of a slave boxer who makes money for his master, but ends up in poverty has a number of parallels in the examples of famous athletes that also found themselves in poverty after they retired, which includes Ali.

Sports on the slave plantations also served the practical purpose of distracting slaves. In his autobiography Frederick Douglass pointed out that the function of sports on the slave plantations was to distract the slaves and keep them from rebelling:

> The days between Christmas and New Year's day are allowed as holidays; and, accordingly, we were not required to perform any labor, more than to feed and take care of the stock. This time we regarded as our own, by the grace of our masters; and we therefore used or abused it nearly as we pleased [...] But by far the larger part engaged in such sports and merriments as playing ball, wrestling, running foot-races, fiddling, dancing, and drinking whisky; and this latter mode of spending the time was by far the most agreeable to the feelings of our masters. A slave who would work during the holidays was considered by our masters as scarcely deserving them. He was regarded as one who rejected the favor of his master. It was deemed a disgrace not to get drunk at Christmas; and he was regarded as lazy indeed, who had not provided himself with the necessary means, during the year, to get whisky enough to last him through Christmas.
>
> From what I know of the effect of these holidays upon the slave, I believe them to be among the most effective means in the hands of the slaveholder in keeping down the spirit of insurrection. Were the slaveholders at once to abandon this practice, I have not the slightest doubt it would lead to an immediate insurrection among the slaves. These holidays serve as conductors, or safety-valves, to carry off the rebellious spirit

146

of enslaved humanity.

The role of the African athlete on the slave plantation was essentially not a revolutionary one. It was a role that helped to enrich the slave master, while at the same time serving to help pacify the other slaves on the plantation through entertainment. I want to clarify this before actually addressing the topic of Muhammad Ali to demonstrate that Ali, as an athlete, was working in a profession that has historically not been a revolutionary one. This may help us to understand some of the limitations of Ali as a political figure. Unlike Malcolm X or Martin Luther King, Ali was not primarily an activist or organizer within the community. He was primarily an athlete who made his living fighting other people in the ring. Ali was certainly vocal about the issue of racism in America and he used his platform as an athlete to preach the message of Elijah Muhammad, but that was truly the extent of Ali's involvement in the civil rights movement of the 1960s.

At the height of his boxing career Muhammad Ali was a hero in the African American community. Many saw in Ali a man that had confidently stood up to white supremacy and someone who was vocal and outspoken about the issues that impacted the African American community. In a sense, Ali's victories in the ring were victories for the black masses. Ali was that rare athlete that seemed to have transcended the realm of sports and took on a political significance. Yet behind this image of a confident, vocal, and fearless champion of the black masses, the reality was that Ali always remained a boxer. That was what he was best at. When it came to his political positions Ali was always someone who followed orders and did what he was told without question.

It may be strange to think of a man who was known for his confident and brash denominator as someone who often slavishly followed orders, but that is precisely what he did. Ali is well-known for the courageous stance he took on the Vietnam War, but the reality is that he did nothing different than any other Muslim was expected to do in that situation. Elijah Muhammad was himself jailed for a period of time for draft evasion during World War II. The Nation of Islam's position on wars was that even when drafted they would refuse to go. Malcolm X explained:

> As Muslims, we don't go to war. We don't get drafted. We don't join anybody's army. We don't teach you not to go because they'd put us in jail for sedition. I would never tell you not to go. I wouldn't be that dumb. But I sure will tell you, if you're dumb enough to go, that's up to you.

This is not to downplay or take away from the significance or bravery of Ali's stand against the Vietnam War. Ali gave up the money, fame, and prestige that went along with being the heavyweight champion of the world, choosing a prison sentence instead. That decision took much courage and conviction. With that being said, the reality is that Ali did not take a position that was not expected of other Muslims. This was merely Ali following the orders of Elijah Muhammad. This is significant because after this Ali never again became such a vocal critic of American foreign policy. After Ali got his boxing license reinstated his main concern was boxing, but Ali did very little to involve himself in the African American struggle beyond simply being a member of the Nation of Islam. Ali never truly transcended the sport of boxing to become a real leader in the community.

Ali was the same guy who abandoned his friend Malcolm X in favor of the Nation of Islam. Malcolm had supported and sided with Ali at a time when the Nation of Islam was distancing itself from the boxer. In fact, prior to Ali joining the Nation of Islam, the Nation of Islam paid no attention to sports to the point that when Malcolm X first met Ali he had no idea who Ali was. After Malcolm died, Ali stayed with the Nation of Islam. A number of people commented on the fact that the Nation of Islam was apparently using Ali to exploit the fame and money that an athlete of his caliber brought to the Nation of Islam. This certainly was not a reciprocal relationship because when Muhammad Ali, who donated much of his money to the Nation of Islam, fell into a difficult financial situation and was forced to continue boxing he did not receive the support of the Nation of Islam. When Ali explained his intentions to return to the ring to Howard Cosell in a public interview, Elijah Muhammad criticized Ali.

Elijah Muhammad responded by suspending Ali and stripping him of his name. Elijah Muhammad accused Ali of having a love for "sport and play," and he claimed that Ali "stepped down off the spiritual platform of Islam to go and see if he can make money in the sport world." Unlike Malcolm, Ali remained loyal to Elijah Muhammad right up until Elijah Muhammad's death in 1975. Wallace Deen Muhammad took over the Nation of Islam and moved the organization towards Sunni Islam. This was when Ali also converted to becoming a Sunni Muslim. This was not a move that Ali made on his own, like Malcolm had done. Michael Ezra explained that the Nation of Islam was "an organization that bled him [Ali] dry and then cast him aside." Despite this, Ali remained blindly loyal to the Nation of Islam until the very end. It was apparent to outside observers that the Nation of Islam was exploiting Ali for his money and fame, but Ali himself had not perceived this.

The other sad reality of the situation is that Elijah Muhammad never seemed to have appreciated Muhammad Ali in the manner that Malcolm did. Malcolm stated that the white media was worried about black people identifying with Ali "because they'd have Negroes walking around the street saying 'I'm the greatest.'" Before Ali joined the Nation of Islam, Malcolm had said that he believed that "Cassius is in a better position than anyone else to restore a sense of racial pride to, not only our people in this country, but all over the world." Elijah Muhammad never expressed the same confidence in Ali's abilities. Elijah Muhammad did not even publicly embrace Ali until Ali had won the championship. Despite this, Ali sided with Elijah Muhammad against Malcolm. When asked if he had split with Malcolm, Ali replied that Malcolm was "not big enough to be called a split." Ali was implying that Malcolm was so insignificant to the movement that Malcolm leaving the movement was not worthy to be called a split. Ali went so far to state that "Malcolm X and anybody else who attacks or talks about attacking Elijah Muhammad will die." Statements such as this contributed to the environment that ultimately led to Malcolm being assassinated by members of the Nation of Islam.

Ali never had the awareness or consciousness that Malcolm had. We see this in the way both men approached the situation in the Congo. Unlike Malcolm X, who was closely following the events that unfolded in the Congo following the assassination of Patrice Lumumba, Ali seemed completely unaware of the situation there. He happily fought George Foreman in a fight that was dubbed the "Rumble in the Jungle," which took place in the Congo (at the time named Zaire). At no point did Ali acknowledge or raise any concerns over Mobutu's dictatorship in Zaire. Although Ali won that fight, it was really Mobutu who benefitted the most from the fight. Dave Saltonstall explained:

> Mobutu put up $10 million in government funds about 3% of Zaire's annual budget to guarantee the purses. In exchange, he reaped a percentage of the fight's profits, which he deposited under his name in a Panamanian account, investigators would later learn. In traveling to Africa, many now believe that Ali unwittingly helped legitimize Mobutu's rule and foster an image of Zaire as a friendly, stable nation that could be trusted.

With the influence of the Nation of Islam no longer behind him, Ali's political stances and his position as a spokesman for issues impacting African people also declined to the point that he was even being used as a pawn to represent American interests in Africa. The 1980 Olympics were held in Moscow in the Soviet Union. The year before the Soviet Union invaded Afghanistan and in response to this President Jimmy Carter announced that the United States would boycott the Moscow Games. Muhammad Ali had already announced that his amateur sport club would boycott the Moscow Olympics in response to the Soviet Union's invasion of Afghanistan. Ali, like the Carter administration, was publicly critical of the Soviet Union's actions and this, combined with Ali's popularity in Africa, made him, in the eyes of President Carter, a great candidate to persuade African governments into supporting the boycott of the Moscow Games. Ali was sent on a diplomatic mission to Tanzania, Kenya, Senegal, Nigeria, and Liberia.

Although it was Carter who approved the decision, it was Arthur Lewis (Director of African Affairs for the International Communications Agency), Malvin Whitfield (Regional and Youth Sports Officer in Africa for the same organization), and Bryant Salter (Vice Consul, American Consulate, Douala, Cameroon) that initially came up with the idea to send Ali based on Ali's popularity in Africa. Carter's decision was met with some criticism from the press and from some within Congress. Representative Robert Bauman stated:

> Mr. Speaker, until recently, I thought nothing the Carter administration does could surprise me. But the President has sent Muhammad Ali on a delicate diplomatic mission to Africa. While it is not true that the President will ask Cyrus Vance to fight Sugar Ray Leonard, it is clear that the administration has brought us into a new age of diplomacy.

The consensus was that this was a terrible diplomatic move on the part of the Carter administration, although in hindsight it was more or less a moderate success rather than a failure. It was certainly a regrettable move on Ali's part. Throughout the 1960s, Ali was seen as a militant and radical figure in the struggle for black rights. He was a member of the Nation of Islam and was outspoken on a number of issues that impacted the black community. Moreover, he took a stance against the Vietnam War that resulted in him being stripped of the heavyweight championship and imprisoned. By 1980, however, Ali was now essentially reduced to a pawn of the Carter administration. Ali was rightfully outraged over the Soviet aggression against Afghanistan, but he was also completely out of touch with the frustrations of many Africans against America's treatment of the apartheid issue in South Africa.

Ali's tour got off to a rough start in Tanzania. President Julius

Nyerere had criticized America's call for a boycott of the Moscow Olympics because the American government had ignored African calls for stricter trade sanctions against South Africa. Many African nations had boycotted the 1976 Olympic Games in Montreal in protest of the apartheid regime. Furthermore, the Soviet Union had been supporting liberation movements in South Africa and other nations—a fact that Ali was unaware of. Not only did Ali have to deal with this issue, but also the fact that many in Tanzania questioned why America had sent a boxer to engage in diplomatic discussions. One Tanzanian official even questioned whether or not America would have sent Chris Evert to London to talk with the English.

It did not help Ali's case that he was not properly informed on the political situation in Africa. Not only was Ali unaware of the fact that the Soviet Union had provided aid for many African liberation groups, but he was also unaware that America had failed to support the boycott of the 1976 Montreal Olympics. Ali defended himself by claiming that he was "not representing America." He further argued that anyone who respected freedom would be offended by the Soviets invading another country. Ali also declared "I'm nobody's Uncle Tom." It is ironic that a boxer, who so often had ridiculed other boxers as Uncle Toms, was now forced to defend himself against the same accusations. Despite Ali's claims, he was still viewed by many as being a government puppet. During a meeting with Minister of Youth and Culture, Chediel Mgonja, Ali was given a note which described him as "an agent of Jimmy Carter's racist imperialist policies." President Nyerere ultimately refused to meet with Ali, much to Ali's disappointment.

President Leopold Senghor was very receptive of Ali. During their meeting the two even shared poetry together, but Senghor did not comply with America's boycott. Senghor was critical of the invasion of Afghanistan, but he also asserted that Senegal would compete in the Olympics because he did not believe in mixing sports with politics. In fact, Senegal had competed in the 1976 Montreal Games despite the African boycott.

Despite the fact that Nyerere and President Alhaji Shehu Shagari of Nigeria had snubbed Ali, and Senghor sent athletes to the Olympics, Ali did manage some success during his tour of Africa. Ali met with President Daniel arap Moi of Kenya, who was supportive of the boycott. Kenya did not send athletes to Moscow. President William Tolbert of Liberia also supported the boycott, although a few months later he was deposed and the new regime decided to send athletes to Moscow. As pointed out before, Senghor decided to send athletes to Moscow, but he was also supportive of Ali's endeavors and had opposed the Soviet invasion of Afghanistan.

Although not an abject failure, Ali's tour of Africa was certainly an ill-advised one. Ali was unaware of Africa's own grievances with the United States or the fact that the Soviet Union had been supporting some of the independence movements in Africa. Moreover, some resented that the United States chose to send a boxer on a diplomatic mission. The Carter administration had assumed that Ali's popularity among Africans would help to sway public opinion in favor of America's Olympic boycott, but Ali's experience in Africa only left Ali feeling disappointed and discouraged.

After this disappointing venture in Africa, Ali returned to the ring again. This was another ill-advised move on Ali's part, but Ali needed the money. Ali was severely beaten in his fight with Larry Holmes in what was a painfully one-sided fight. Despite the fact that it was apparent in his fight with Holmes that Ali had no business being in the ring, Ali returned in 1981 for a final match with Trevor Berbick. Ali lost this fight and retired for good afterwards. By the time Ali left boxing he was essentially a shell of his former self. Ali's health was rapidly declining and he was struggling financially. At the time of his retirement, Ali was on his third marriage and had a large number of children to support. Ezra explains:

During the 1980s Ali was something of a laughing stock, considered to be punchdrunk and pathetic, parodied mercilessly on shows like Saturday Night Live and In Living

Color as an over-the-hill halfwit. He had little money and was in rapidly declining health, more removed from public consciousness than ever.

Further proof of the decline in Ali's significance as a political figure was his support for Ronald Reagan's presidential campaign in the 1980s. Reagan was a man who stood on the opposite side of Ali during the Vietnam War. In speaking of Ali, Reagan, who was then governor of California, stated: "That draft dodger will never fight in my state, period." Reagan gladly accepted Ali's endorsement, however. That Ali could endorse such a man for president really demonstrates how radically different the Ali of the 1980s was from the Ali that took a stance against the Vietnam War. By the 1980s Ali was neither the flashy and graceful fighter that he had been in the 1960s, nor was he the voice for black liberation that he had been when he was with the Nation of Islam. Ali's departure from the Nation of Islam was also a departure from the pro-black position that Ali once had, and without the boxing skills that he once had Ali had become, as Ezra stated, someone who was removed from the public consciousness.

Ali was someone who could very well have been an influential leader within the black community. He certainly had the speaking ability and the charisma, but Ali never used his position or influence in the community to create a position for himself as a leader. Instead, he was intent on boxing much longer than he should have, which resulted in the rapid decline of his health. Moreover, Ali had no real political understanding, which allowed him to be exploited at the convenience of political leaders. As a member of the Nation of Islam he unquestionably accepted the authority of Elijah Muhammad, even after Malcolm had broken away from the organization and exposed many of the faults within the movement. Ali unquestionably fought in Zaire to the benefit of Mobutu and he unquestionably represented Jimmy Carter in Africa. Most puzzling of all was his support for Ronald Reagan, a man who criticized Ali's stance on Vietnam. Ali may have been an excellent fighter inside of the ring, but Ali's legacy outside of the ring as a political figure left much to be desired from a man who wielded so much influence and fame. As was mentioned, the role of the black athlete was not created to be a revolutionary one that creates social change. Ali is easily the most politically relevant athlete of his era (which was an era that included the likes of Jim Brown, John Carlos, Tommie Smith and Kareem Abdul-Jabbar), but Ali was unable to fully transcend the limited social role of professional athletes.

Selected References:

Dave Saltonstall, "Dictator Won Ali Bout," *New York Daily News*, April 1997.

Daniel Bennett Coy, "Imagining Dissent: Muhammad Ali Daily Newspapers, and the State, 1966-1971," Master's Thesis, University of Tennessee, 2004.

Maureen Smith, "*Muhammad Speaks* and Muhammad Ali: Intersections of the Nation of Islam and Sport in the 1960s" *International Sports Studies*, Volume 22, 2000.

Michael Ezra, "Muhammad Ali's deification shows an America reluctant to confront its past," *The Guardian*, January 2012.

Stephen R. Wenn & Jeffery P. Wenn, "Muhammad Ali and the Convergence of Olympic Sport and U.S. Diplomacy in 1980: A Reassessment from Behind the Scenes at the U.S. State Department," *The International Journal of Olympic Studies* Volume II, 1993, pp. 45-66

7

SLAVERY IN GREECE AND ROME AS A PARALLEL TO NEW WORLD SLAVERY

"One is able to endure even the shame of slaves in arms. For although slaves are persons who have been made subject to punishment in every possible way by some stroke of misfortune, they are still a type of human being, albeit an inferior type, and they are capable of being initiated into the benefits of the freedom that we enjoy."
-Florus

In 1492, Christopher Columbus sailed to the Caribbean. This began a scramble to colonize what the Europeans called "The New World." In reality, this world may have been new to Columbus, but it was populated with people long before Columbus got there. In this New World, Europeans established what will be referred to here as "slave economies" that were largely dependent on the importation and forced labor of Africans. Having virtually wiped out the indigenous population in many areas of the New World, Europeans eventually turned to importing Africans to work as slave labor—also keep in mind that before Africans were imported as slave labor, Europeans were imported as indentured laborers to work on the plantations of the New World. The importation of enslaved people from the African continent became a business unto itself. Once imported, against their wills, into the Americas, Africans were then used as labor on the plantations to cultivate products such as cotton and sugar, or mining gold in the case of Brazil. These are just some examples, but enslaved people were used in other roles as well. From the unpaid labor of African people European nations enriched themselves greatly.

Such slave societies were not entirely new to Europeans. The reality is that the slave economies do have a precedent in European history. In Greece and Rome, particularly, slavery played an integral economic function. Whereas the slavery in the New World became a racial caste system in which Europeans dominated Africans, the slavery in Greece and Rome was largely a system of Europeans enslaving other Europeans. Nevertheless, slaves in Greece and Rome were treated horribly in many instances and had essentially no rights.

Before getting into the topic of slavery in Greece and Rome, it should be pointed out that slavery was an institution that existed in various forms throughout human history. It is not something that is particular to European societies. With that being said, it should also be pointed out that what the term "slave economy" refers to is an economic system which is largely dependent on the sale of slaves and the usage of slave labor. The contrast can be understood when comparing Europe between the 1400s and 1800s, with that of West Africa during the same time frame.

The Economics of African Slavery

The system of slavery that was established by the Europeans in the New World was one based largely on race. Africans were taken against their wills from their homelands and brought to the New World. There they were forced to work under brutal and inhumane conditions. The societies that they lived in offered them little if any rights largely based on the fact that Africans were viewed as being sub-human. The justification for subjugating African people was that they were savage and uncivilized, and needed to be introduced to Christianity to save their souls. These slave societies determined that solely on the basis of their race were African people to be subjected to slavery and treated like property.

Africans had an internal system of slavery as well, but this system was different in a number of ways. Firstly, African societies did not have slave economies such as that in the New World. War captives, criminals, and other individuals that found themselves in a circumstance of servitude were often sold to European traders, but this only benefited the traders, which were most often the elites in Africa or mulatto traders. Overall, however, the economies of African societies were not based on the use of slave labor. The slave trade was so profitable for certain African kingdoms that some of them, such as Dahomey, were resistant towards European attempts to abolish the slave trade because the slave trade became the basis of Dahomey's economy, but Dahomey was not a "slave economy" in the sense that New World economies were.

Slavery in Africa also was not a permanent caste system as it was in the New World. The following quote explains five of the ways in which one was sold into slavery to the Europeans:

> African natives became merchantable slaves in any one of five ways. They were criminals sold by the native chief as punishment; or they were individuals sold by themselves or their families in time of famine; or they were persons kidnapped either by European slavers or, more often, by native gangs; or they have been slaves in Africa and were sold by their masters; or else they were prisoners of war.

Pay attention to the fact that there is no mention of people being born to be sold as slaves. This is important because in New World slavery and in Greco-Roman slavery, those born of slave parents were also themselves enslaved. This served to reproduce the slave population in those societies. In Africa, however, those who were born from enslaved parents were typically born as free people and integrated into the society as citizens—this was neither the case in New World slavery or in slavery in Athens. There are also examples—such as Jaja of Opobo and Sakura of Mali—in which formerly enslaved Africans rose to become kings in or nearby the very nations where they were enslaved. There is no parallel to this in New World slavery, except in Haiti where slaves overthrew their slave masters through revolution and established a republic of their own, but to rise to power the slaves had to overturn the entire social and political structure of the society. There is also no parallel to this in Greece and Rome, where slaves also rebelled in an attempt to obtain their freedom.

Domestic slaves that belonged to their masters' households in African societies had many of the rights that were so often denied to slaves in both the New World, and in Greece and Rome. Walter Rodney explains:

> They could not be sold, except for serious offences, they had their own plots of land and/or rights to a proportion of the fruits of their labour; they could marry; their children had rights of inheritance; and if born of one free parent, often acquired a new status. Such individuals could rise to positions of great trust, including that of chief.

Finally, as was pointed out, slavery in Africa was not a major economic institution. Boniface Obichere explains that slavery in Asante (alternatively known as Ashanti) and Dahomey was more a social institution than an economic one:

> In Asante and Dahomey, slavery was a social and political institution and not primarily an economic affair. Differences existed between the categories of slavery in Asante and Dahomey but the contrasts were negligible except in the cases of the akyere and the kan nou mon vodunsi. Slaves were employed in domestic service as well as in military and political service in both kingdoms. There appears to have been a larger number of slaves in Dahomey than in Asante. In both kingdoms, slaves were used for the purpose of replenishing the population and for preventing the extinction of some family lines. Slaves were in evidence more in social occasions as adornment and retinue for their masters than in the economic sphere. Upward mobility into the ranks of freemen was available to slaves in both kingdoms. There are cases of ex-slaves who rose to great fame.

Asante and Dahomey are notable here because during the period of the slave trade those were two kingdoms that were deeply involved in the trade of war captives. They were among what historian

Henry Louis Gates termed "slave kingdoms" in West Africa. This term obscures the reality of slavery in both kingdoms in that slavery was not a primary economic function in either kingdom. As stated before, the slave trade may have enriched certain rulers and traders within the kingdom and there was a sizeable slave population, but as Lansiné Kaba explains: "Despite the size of the slave population in Ashanti, Dahomey, and other states, free-labor farming rather than slavery was the basis of the economy." Therefore, Asante and Dahomey did not have "slave economies" as Greece, Rome, and the New World colonies did.

Walter Rodney cites the example of the Manes after their invasion into Sierra Leone in 1545. This massive invasion naturally produced a large number of war captives, many of which were sold to the Portuguese slavers. Rodney notes that so many captives were taken after this invasion that some of the ships had to reject captives because they simply did not have the space to hold anymore. The Sape people, which were among those that were conquered by the Manes, were recruited as soldiers and the others were sold. Rodney explains that the Manes sold as many Sapes as they could to "make the restless population manageable." In other words, some of the conquered Sapes were used as soldiers, but the Manes generally did not have any use for a sizeable slave population, which a slave economy would require.

This is not to defend slavery in Africa or to suggest that there were no abuses in the African system of slavery—although even in instances where abuses did occur there were attempts to suppress it, such as in Asante where rulers made laws prohibiting the harsh treatment of slaves. The point is to demonstrate that slavery in Africa was much less severe than what Europeans established in the New World. With this being established, we shall now look at the systems of slavery in Greece and Rome, which actually provides many parallels with the system of slavery in the New World. It should be stated again that slavery in Greece and Rome was not based on a racial caste system, but this was a system that was very ruthless and inhumane in its treatment of slaves. As was the case in the New World, slave resistance in Greece and Rome was common because of this.

Slavery in Greece

A number of Greek city-states were slave societies in which slaves played an important economic function, as well as assisting in warfare. Greek city-states had a significant population of slaves, with some estimates stating that at the time of the Peloponnesian War there were as many as 100,000 slaves in Greece. Peter Hunt explains:

> Overall, slave ownership was more widely distributed among the free than in New World slavery: at the height of Athenian wealth, fully a third of the citizen males probably owned at least one slave; very few owned large numbers of slaves, i.e. over thirty.

In most Greek city-states slaves were chattel which were bought and sold for the use of their labor. In Athens, in particular, slaves had little to no legal rights and social standing. They were not able to own property, could not bring a suit before court, had no legally recognized family relationships, were restricted from religious festivals and lacked the public rights of citizens. Moreover, masters were free to treat their slaves however they saw fit. The abuse of slaves was so widespread that it became the subject of Greek comedy.

The newly freed slaves in Greece often faced the threat of re-enslavement and still owed service to their former master. Moreover, in only rare cases were newly freed slaves able to attain citizenship. There is a specific case of an Athenian lawsuit against a slave named Neaira for unlawfully posing as an Athenian citizen to secure citizenship status for her children. For a child to be considered a citizen they had to be born from citizens. Throughout the proceedings it was determined that Neaira was one of seven slave girls that were purchased by a freedwoman named Nikarete. These slave girls were used as prostitutes by Nikarete. In court, a number of Neaira's clients were listed during the case, including two young men named Timanoridas and Eukrates who decided to buy Neaira because they felt that Nikarete was charging them too much. The two men kept Neaira as a sex slave before growing tired with her. They decided that if she could pay them 20 *mnas*, they would remit the other 10 *mnas* of the 30 *mnas* that they had paid to acquire Neaira in the first place. In essence, they were willing to grant her freedom at a financial loss to themselves.

To pay for this, Neaira sought money from former lovers. Due to the fact that slaves could not legally pay for their own freedom, Neaira had to use a third-party to purchase her freedom. To achieve this she turned to a former client named Phrynion. She gave him the money that she collected, although she did not collect the full 20 *mnas* and Phrynion had to make up the balance with his own money. The outcome of the trial is unclear, but the whole ordeal demonstrated that even freed slaves in Athens did enjoy equal citizenship.

One is reminded of the case of Dred Scott in the United States, which demonstrated that even after an enslaved African was granted freedom they did not necessarily enjoy the rights of citizenship. Scott attempted to sue Eliza Irene Sanford for the freedom of his wife and children. The official ruling by the Supreme Court was that Africans, whether they were free or enslaved, were not American citizens and did not have the right to sue in court. They ruled that Africans had "no rights which the white man was bound to respect." In Athens slavery was not a racial caste system as it was in the United States, but the system was set up so that even if a slave managed to obtain freedom, they still would not be given the same rights as an Athenian citizen.

The militarized Greek city-state of Sparta was maintained through the exploitation of a large population of enslaved peasants that were known as Helots. The Helots were conquered by Sparta and reduced to a servile role. The Helots were not chattel slaves in the sense that they were bought and sold, however. They resembled serfs more than chattel slaves—rather than being owned by particular individuals, Helots belonged to the Spartan state.

Helots had their own villages and homes, but they were bound to whichever parcel of land that they lived on. They were also required to provide a large portion of the output of their labor to their Spartan masters.

Sparta was a militarized state in which boys were practically born to become warriors. At birth male infants were examined to determine whether or not that infant should be raised. Plutarch writes:

> The father did not decide whether to raise a baby; rather he took it and carried it to some place called Lesche where the elders of the tribe sat and examined the infant, and if it were well-built and sturdy, they ordered the father to rear it.

At age 7, Spartan boys were taken from their family and placed in an education that required them to eat and sleep with other boys until they reached the age of 20. Once they reached that age, they became full-time soldiers and would remain in military service until the age of 60. The Helots were also used to develop young boys into soldiers. An elite few of the older boys were assigned to a group known as the Kryptoi. They would be armed with knives and sent to Messenia, where they were forced to survive on their own, mainly through robbing and killing Helots.

Interestingly, the highly militarized nature of Sparta allowed women in Sparta more freedoms than women in other Greek city-states enjoyed. In most Greek city-states, women were legally under the guardianship of a male. They could not own land or inherit property, but the women of Sparta not only owned land, they reportedly controlled as much as 40 percent of Sparta's agricultural terrain by the early 4th century B.C. Moreover, Sparta offered universal education for girls, which was found in none of the other Greek city-states. Much of this was due to the fact that Spartan men spent much of their time at war. Proof of the connection between Sparta's need for a standing military presence to keep Messenia under their control and increased rights for women is the fact that when Sparta lost control of Messenia, the role of women in Sparta reverted to that of women in other Greek city-states.

The Helots, especially the ones from Messenia, tended to be rebellious and made a number of attempts to free themselves in various battles against the Spartans. The Second Messenian War, which was fought in the seventh century B.C., was a failed attempt by the Messenian Helots to achieve freedom from Spartan control. One of these rebellions was so massive that Sparta was forced to seek assistance from allies throughout Greece to put down the rebellion in 490 B.C. Putting down such rebellions occupied so much of Sparta's concerns that some of the treaties that Sparta made with its allies specified that those allies had to assist Sparta if the "slaves rose in rebellion." The Helot discontent with Sparta sometimes benefited Sparta's enemies, especially during the Peloponnesian War. Athens gave Naupactus, a city which they had conquered, to Messenian refugees who had left the Peloponnese. These Messenians became loyal allies of the Athenians during the Peloponnesian War. In another instance, Sparta attempted to promise freedom to several thousand Helots to help in a fight against a Theban led army. The Theban army was attempting to liberate Messenia and many Helots deserted to the Theban cause.

Helot rebellions were a dangerous prospect for Sparta. The Helots outnumbered the Spartans by as much as ten to one. The Spartans saw the Helots as a constant threat and as such brutally repressed the population. This included declaring war on the Messenian Helots annually, regardless of whether or not those Helots had actually rebelled. During these declarations, a Spartan was free to kill a Helot without facing any punishments, regardless of the circumstances around the killing. The Helots were stuck in a constant state of repression and fear.

The Helots made up such a large element in the Spartan army that Herodotus reported that at the Battle of Plataea the Helot soldiers outnumbered the Spartans by seven to one. Spartans also recruited smaller numbers of Helots for distant and long campaigns. Such service did not go unrewarded. Helot soldiers that served in these military engagements were rewarded with freedom from the obligations that were enforced on the Helots. This also served to decrease the likelihood of Helot revolts. The Spartans did not want to leave Peloponnese out of fear of Helot rebellions. Promising freedom to some Helots and sending them to fight distant campaigns worked to co-opt and remove some of the more hostile Helots, while allowing the Spartans to remain nearby to monitor the Helots that were under their control.

Helots also played a significant role in the Battle of Thermopylae, which is easily the most well-known battle in Spartan history. This battle took place in the larger context of Persia's attempt to invade Athens, possibly as punishment for Athens supporting a rebellion against Persia. Emperor Xerxes marched his army towards Greece. In route to Athens, the Persian army passed through a narrow pass known as Thermopylae. A Greek army led by the Spartan king Leonidas confronted the Persians at this pass. The army, which numbered thousands of soldiers, included 300 Spartans.

The battle is remembered for the bravery which the Spartans demonstrated in the conflict. All of the 300 Spartans, including Leonidas, were slain in the battle. Along with the 300 Spartans that were killed, there must have been even more Helots that were also killed by the Persian army. As was standard practice, Helots fought alongside the Spartans during this conflict. The exact number of Helots that fought is unknown, although some estimates place the number of Helots that fought in the battle as high as 900. Despite the loss, the Greeks ultimately won the war and defeated the Persian Empire—the largest empire in the world at that time.

Athens also employed slaves in combat. The most common usage of slaves for Athens was in the Navy, where the majority of slaves served as rowers for the battleships. Rowers did not possess weapons, so these slave rowers were less of a threat than armed slave infantries were. The Peloponnesian War between Sparta and Athens helped to disrupt the practice of slavery in Athens. The Athenians had lost two large navies and were being challenged by the Spartan navy, which was subsidized by the Persian king. By 406 B.C., the Athenian fleet only manned seventy ships, rather than the 100 that they were able to man the year before. They were being outnumbered by the Spartan fleet, which numbered 170.

For the battle of Arginusae against Sparta the Athenians were forced to gather more recruits for naval combat. To achieve this, the Athenians promised not only freedom to their slave rowers, but citizenship as well. Athens would go on to defeat Sparta in Arginusae, destroying about two-thirds of Sparta's fleet. Although Athens would eventually lose the Peloponnesian War in 404 B.C., the victory at Arginusae demonstrated that Athens' tactic of promising freedom and citizenship worked to achieve the intended goal. Nevertheless, this move was surely met with outrage from Athenian slave masters.

Freeing the slaves that fought in Arginusae did not radically change the structure of Athenian society. By the end of the Peloponnesian War, Athens was short of slaves, but Athens continued to be a slave society. This would change following Alexander the Great's conquest of Athens. The Hellenistic kingdoms that emerged from Alexander's conquests were not slave societies, although the Greek elites still owned slaves. The economy changed so that the rural economy was dominated by a peasantry.

Another incident which offered Athenian slaves freedom was when Philip of Macedon defeated Athens and their allies at the battle of Chaeronia in 338 B.C. Out of desperation, the Athenians voted to free and arm their slaves. Athens did not carry through with these measures, however. Philip instead offered Athens a chance to make peace, which they accepted. Hyperides, the man who proposed the idea of arming slaves, was put on trial. His defense was "it was not I who wrote the decree; the battle of Chaeronia did."

Slavery in Rome

Historian Walter Scheidel described Rome as having built "the largest slave society in history." As such, slavery was an integral aspect of Rome's economy. Slaves occupied various positions in Rome. They served as estate managers, field hands, shepherds, hunters, teachers, doctors, soldiers, and gladiators. Slavery was such an integral aspect of the Roman economy that Scheidel describes Rome's economy as a "slave economy" due to the fact that the elites "relied to a significant degree of slave labor to generate surplus and maintain their position of dominance."

In Rome the most common ways of becoming a slave were either being taken captive during a war or being born of a slave mother. Punishment for serious crimes also entailed enslavement and in the early era of the Roman city-states, slavery was a punishment for refusing military service or desertion. Roman law regarded all persons that were on the enemy's side during war as potential slaves. This did not only apply to enemy soldiers, but civilians as well. Very often these captives either became slaves of the state or were auctioned off. For this reason, Rome's military conquests ensured a frequent influx of new slaves into the empire. Much as slavery in the New World, one who was born to an enslaved mother was also a slave, thus there was a process of reproduction within the existing slave population in Rome.

Under Roman law, just as in Athens and in New World slavery, slaves had no legal rights and were treated more like property than people. As such, slaves could be bought and sold, or passed on to an heir following the death of their master. Masters were given complete control over their slaves, to the point that the slave master had the right to kill his slave if he saw fit, although killing or maiming the slave of another person was a punishable offence—akin to the crime of damaging or destroying someone else's property. In cases of severe abuse, a magistrate would reprimand the owner, but this seemed to have been done more as a means to uphold morality among the citizens than out of concern for the plight of the slaves. Over time, slaves were granted more protections under the law. Emperor Antoninus Pius made killing a slave a criminal offence and Emperor Constantine decreed that anyone who killed a slave would be punished as a murderer. Slaves in Rome, just as in Athens, had no rights. They could not own property and had no standing in court. They were not even able to enter into a legally recognized marriage.

Given the often repressive nature of slavery in Rome, it is little surprise that slaves resisted in a number of ways. One of which was running away. A code of Roman laws known as *The Digest* gives a legal definition for what a fugitive slave is. These laws also stipulated that anyone who hid a runaway slave was a thief and would be subject to punishment. Much like in New World slavery, runaway slaves in Rome were considered property and were expected to be returned to the rightful owner of said property. At times runaway slaves managed to create maroon communities of their own, much as Africans in the New World created maroon settlements of their own in places such as Brazil, Haiti, Jamaica, and Surinam.

In other occasions, slaves took a more direct approach by waging war to obtain their freedom. In 198 B.C. there were slave rebellions at Setia and Praeneste. Another slave rebellion broke out in Etruria and was suppressed in 196 B.C. Some of the leaders of this uprising were whipped and then crucified. There was also the case of a man named Titus Vettius Minutius, who came from a wealthy father and held the rank of *eques* (Roman elites who ranked just below senators in prestige). Minutius fell in love with a slave girl and attempted to purchase her from the girl's master. Minutius managed to get the girl's master to allow him to buy her freedom. The problem was that Minutius simply did not have the resources to pay for the girl's freedom. Minutius decided to acquire weapons and incite 400 of his slaves in rebellion. This revolt was crushed. Minutius and some of the other rebels committed suicide to avoid being captured. The three largest slave uprisings in Rome were known collectively as the Servile Wars.

There are common themes that run through each of these three wars, which provide an important understanding of how slavery worked in Rome. One such theme is that in all three cases slaves were compelled to rebel due to the poor treatment that they received at the hands of their slave masters. In all three cases, Rome also seemed to have underestimated the slaves. Indeed, the thought of waging a war against enslaved people seemed beneath the dignity of the Romans. Florus expressed such a viewpoint when he wrote:

> Even if we fought against our own Italian allies—itself an impious act—at least we fought with free and freeborn men. But who can even bear the thought, and not be greatly disturbed by it, of wars waged by slaves against the leading people of the civilized world?

The first Servile slave war lasted from 135 to 132 B.C. This revolt, which took place on the island of Sicily, was led by a Syrian born slave known as Eunus, who was known as a magician. The revolt broke out in the city of Enna, where slaves were extremely maltreated. Two of the most notable of these slave masters were a wealthy and arrogant slave owner named Damophilus and his wife Megallis, who were both known to treat their slaves inhumanly. The cause of this uprising seemed to have been the harsh manner in which the masters treated their slaves. Diodorus Siculus explains:

> Since they were convinced that the slaves deserved only minimum care, they gave them the least possible food and clothing. Most of the slaves were forced to provide their own livelihood by becoming bandits.

The governors of Sicily attempted to prevent the spread of these bandit gangs, but with little success. Diodorus Siculus explained that as these gangs spread the result was that everywhere in Sicily was filled with murder. Fed up with the beatings and other hardships that they endured, other slaves began plotting an uprising. Among the conspirators was a Syrian born slave named Eunus, who became the leader of this revolt. Eunus was known as a magician and wonder worker, which helped him to amass large support from the other slaves. Florus writes of Eunus:

> A certain Syrian named Eunus—the very magnitude of the disasters he caused makes us remember him—by feigning a sort of crazed madness and tossing about his locks of hair in his worship of the Syrian goddess, incited the slaves to arms and to freedom, pretending that he had received such a command from the divine spirit.

The slaves unleashed their frustrations on their masters and other freed people with relentless violence. One account of the revolt from Diodorus Siculus depicted the chaos and destruction that was caused by the uprising:

> Never had there been such a great uprising of slaves as then arose in Sicily. Because of it, cities fell into terrible disasters, and countless men and women, along with their children experienced the gravest misfortunes. The whole island seemed about to fall into the hands of fugitive slaves, who measured the extent of their power by excesses of the misfortunes that were suffered by free persons.

Diodorus Siculus recorded some of the acts of violence committed by these rebellious slaves:

> Breaking into the houses in the city, the rebel slaves instituted a general slaughter, not even sparing the suckling infants among the inhabitants. Tearing them from their mothers' breasts, they dashed the infants to the ground. One cannot actually say in words what they did to the women themselves—and with their husbands looking on—what terrible acts of outrage and utter lewdness were committed on them.

Eunus was chosen as the king of the rebels based on his ability to work wonders with his powers and because he was the one who started the revolt. As the ruler of the rebels, Eunus decreed that all the inhabitants of Enna who were taken prisoner were to be executed, with the exception of those who were skilled in manufacturing weapons. Those people were placed in chains and forced to work in workshops. Damophilus was taken before an assembly where he attempted to save himself by convincing the crowd of his innocence. Hermeias and Zeuxis, two men who were in the assembly, grew impatient and killed Damophilus. Megallis was given to the female slaves. They tortured her and then threw Megallis off of a nearby cliff. Eunus also killed his own masters, Antigense and Pytho.

At the time that this was taking place, there was another revolt of runaway slaves on the island, which was led by a Cilician named Kleon. Kleon was "a herder of horses and a man who habitually robbed travelers and committed murders all over the place." Kleon was inspired to begin a revolt of his own by the success of Eunus. He persuaded some nearby slaves to join him in his attack on Acragas and the surrounding countryside. Kleon eventually joined Eunus' uprising and was made a general within Eunus' forces.

The uprising was finally suppressed by Publius Rupilius. Kleon died in combat with a few men. His body was put on public display. Komas, who was believed to be the brother of Kleon, was captured and taken before Rupilius for questioning where Komas apparently took his own life rather than face the punishment that awaited him for being involved in the uprising. Eunus and a thousand of his men attempted to hide in "steep and rugged terrain." Realizing the hopelessness of their situation, Eunus' men committed suicide. Eunus hid himself in a cave with four other men. The five of them were discovered and dragged out of the cave. Eunus was placed in detention where he was ravaged by lice before dying.

Sicily was devastated in the aftermath of the slave uprising. Florus records:

> Leaving no evil undone, Eunus even adorned himself with royal insignia. He inflicted a devastation on fortified places, villages, and towns that was pitiful to behold. Finally, in the ultimate shame of the war, he even captured the army camps of Roman praetors.

Florus' account attests to the general negative manner in which the Romans remembered Eunus' revolt. His memory was connected with the destruction and evils which he is said to have done. It seemed particularly shameful to the Romans that Sicily was "far more cruelly devastated" by slaves than it had even been in the war with Carthage. Eunus was held in such low-esteem that in his prosecution of Gaius Verres, a former Roman governor of Sicily, the Roman senator Cicero argued that Verres' conduct was even worse than that of the rebel slaves, whom Cicero described as beings of "wickedness rather piety". Cicero continued to explain to Verres:

> They [the rebel slaves] were less fugitives from their masters than you are from what is lawful and right. They were less savage by speech and origin than you are by birth and character. They were less the enemies of humanity than you are of the gods.

The Second Servile War took place from 104 to 100 B.C. This uprising was sparked by a proclamation that forbade freed Romans from being wrongfully taken into slavery. Rome was attempting to build up recruitments for their army, but the king of Bithynia was unable to achieve this because too many of the men in his kingdom were kidnapped and taken into slavery. The Roman Senate passed a law that was to protect free people from being taken into slavery. This measure freed more than 800 people in a matter of a few days. The problem with this new decree was that slaves in Sicily began yearning for their freedom as well.

Desiring their freedom, thirty slaves that belonged to two wealthy brothers revolted. Led by a man named Varius, they slit their masters' throats during the night as they were asleep. They then went to neighboring farms, inciting the slaves there to join the uprising. By the first night of the revolt, their numbers already exceeded 120. Licinius Nerva marched against the rebelling slaves, but with no success.

Nerva was the governor of the island of Sicily at the time of the uprising. Nerva's own policy concerning slaves played a role in the tensions that led to the uprising in the first place. Nerva made public a notice which stated that he would help any slaves that had charges to bring against their master. Cassius Dio explains that

"Nerva did this either because he had learned that some slaves were not being fairly treated in certain respects or because he was seeking personal gain, for he was the type of man who was not immune to bribery." Slaves were in fact being treated unfairly and many of them brought charges against their masters. The slave masters, however, refused to concede to any of the slaves' demands. Nerva was caught in-between the conflict between slave and slave master, and decided that he would no longer hear any of the complaints that the slaves had. Nerva hoped that this would defuse the situation, but it only made matters worse, as Cassius Dio explains:

> The slaves, however, who were afraid of their masters because they had dared raise their voices against them, gathered together in a group and by agreement among themselves, turned to banditry.

The rebels formed a government of their own in Sicily and selected a man named Salvius to be their king. Under the command of Salvius, the slaves raided the countryside, acquiring horses and other animals in the process. Diodorus Siculus describes the rebel onslaught against Morgantina:

> Without warning, they suddenly fell on the strong city of Morgantina and subjected it to savage and unceasing assaults. With about ten thousand Italian allied troops as well as soldiers from Sicily under his command, Nerva, the governor, started a forced march in the middle of the night to bring help to the city.

As the rebels were preoccupied with their siege of the city, Nerva attacked their camp, which was only guarded by a few men. Nerva captured the camp and then advanced to Morgantina. The rebels in turn attacked Nerva's forces as they approached the city. As the rebels gained the upper hand in the conflict, Nerva's forces fled the battlefield. Salvius issued a proclamation sparing the lives of Roman soldiers who put down their weapons. This proclamation increased the number of those Roman soldiers who ran away from the battlefield, rather than face death in attempting to defeat the rebels. Salvius was not only able to retake his camp, but he also came into possession of many weapons. This success also doubled Salvius' forces, as more men flocked to his support. Diodorus Siculus writes: "Because of the humane proclamation of the king, no more than six hundred Italians and Sicilians died in the battle, while more than four thousand were taken prisoner."

Salvius made a second attempt at taking Morgantina. This time he issued a proclamation which promised to free all of the slaves in the city. The slave masters in Morgantina countered this by promising freedom to any slave who fought to defend the city. This worked, as the slaves chose their masters' offer and helped to repel the siege. The Roman governor reneged on the promise of freedom for the slaves that helped to defend Morgantina, however. This caused most of the slaves to run away and join the rebels.

In the rural areas around Segesta and Lilybaeum, a man named Athenion was inciting slaves to rebel. Athenion was of Cilician origin. He was a domain manager for two wealthy brothers. He first managed to persuade two hundred slaves to join him. He then won the support of slaves in neighboring farms, so that within the span of five days he had more than 1,000 slaves under his command. Florus describes Athenion's onslaught as follows:

> He raised an army that was just as large as that of his demented predecessor, but he conducted his operations with even greater savagery, as if he were seeking vengeance for Eunus. Athenion plundered villages, towns, and fortresses. He vented his rage on loyal slaves in these communities with even greater violence than he did on their masters, since he considered the slaves to be traitors.

Athenion was selected by his people to be their ruler. Diodorus Siculus records that he managed them differently from other rebel groups:

175

He did not accept all slaves who went into revolt, but turned only the best of them into soldiers. He forced the others to remain at their former tasks and had each of them take care of their own household managerial tasks and work assignments.

Athenion was also someone who was known to be very skilled at predicting future events from the stars. He claimed that through the stars he was able to determine that the gods told him he would one day become king of all of Sicily. After building a massive army, Athenion laid siege to the city of Lilybaeum. This assault was unsuccessful and Athenion retreated.

In the meantime, Salvius managed to conquer Morgantina and renamed himself King Tryphon. Tryphon was now attempting to take Triokala and requested for Athenion to become one of his generals. Athenion accepted this offer, which came as a surprise to some who expected Athenion to contest Tryphon's claim as the leader of the rebel slaves. Had the two come into conflict with each other the slave uprising would have surely destroyed itself, but instead Athenion decided to serve as Tryphon's general. Tryphon then marched to Triokala. As they approached the city, distrust seemed to emerge between the two rebel slave leaders and Tryphon ordered Athenion to be placed in detention.

Triokala became the stronghold for Tryphon, who lavishly adorned the city and "made it even more impregnable than it had been." The Roman Senate appointed Lucius Licinius Lucullus to confront the rebels. Lucullus was the commander who crushed the previously mentioned revolt of Minutius, which occurred shortly before the Second Servile War. Tryphon was also preparing for war against the Romans. He released Athenion from detention. Tryphon's plan was to confront the Romans at Triokala, but Athenion advised Tryphon to confront the Romans in open terrain, rather than accepting a siege and trapping themselves in the city. The rebels went with Athenion's plan and established a camp outside of the city.

Their confrontation with the Romans was a bloody one, with many men being killed on both sides. In the battle Athenion killed a large number of men, but was unable to continue fighting after

176

being wounded in both knees, before suffering a third wound. The rebels lost their morale and ran from the battle field. Athenion also managed to evade capture by pretending to be dead and then escaping at night. This was a crushing defeat for the rebels. After the Roman victory, Tryphon and his supporters ran away from the battlefield. Many men were killed in their attempt to escape. In total, at least 20,000 rebels were killed. Diodorus Siculus describes:

> If the Roman general had followed them in hot pursuit, it would have been easy to kill them all. The general body of the slaves was so downcast and depressed that some of them even urged that they should return to their masters and submit themselves again voluntarily to their masters' authority. But the opposite opinion—that they should fight to the death and should not surrender to their enemies— won the day.

Nine days after the battle, the Roman general arrived at Triokala and launched their attack. The rebels managed to successfully repel this attack and forced the Roman general to withdraw in defeat. This victory helped to embolden the rebels. For his failure, the Roman general was punished. Gaius Servilius was sent to put down the rebellion after Lucullus' failure. Like Lucullus before him, Servilius failed to quell the slave uprising and was punished for his failures. As the Romans struggled to put down this revolt, Tryphon died, leaving Athenion as his successor.

The Romans dispatched Manius Aquillius to repress the revolt. Whereas the other generals had failed, Aquillius finally managed to crush the revolt. Athenion confronted Aquillius in hand-to-hand combat. Aquillius managed to kill Athenion, but suffered an injury in the process. Once he recovered, Aquillius continued his campaign against the rebels. Aquillius crushed the rebellion, although a thousand rebels still remained, under the leadership of a general named Satyros. At first Aquillius attempted to defeat the remaining rebels by force, but he later negotiated with them. The terms were that the slaves would be exempt from execution, and instead be taken to Rome where Aquillius intended to have them fight as gladiators in combat against wild animals. Rather than accepting this offer, the slaves killed each other. After killing the last man, Satyros then took his own life. This ended a slave rebellion that had lasted nearly four years. This would be the longest lasting of the three major slave wars in Roman history.

One of the functions of slaves in Rome was as gladiators who fought each other (sometimes to the death) for the entertainment of audiences. These gladiators were highly trained warriors who were very skilled with the use of a variety of weapons. For this reason, gladiators were viewed, and rightfully so, as potentially dangerous threats. For this reason, gladiators were usually kept under close guard.

The slaves who were trained as gladiators often resisted their fate in a number of ways, which sometimes included suicide. Seneca noted an example of this when he wrote about one of the gladiators who killed himself during a training session at a gladiator school:

> In the latrine, he picked up the stick tipped with a sponge which was provided for the purposes of cleaning one's obscene parts. Then, jamming the whole thing down his throat, he blocked his windpipe and suffocated himself to death.

In another occasion, twenty-nine Saxon slaves committed suicide by strangling themselves rather than participate in the gladiatorial games. Symmachus wrote a letter to his brother complaining about these slaves and described them as "worse than Spartacus himself." This letter was written more than 400 years after the uprising that was led by Spartacus and it demonstrated the place that Spartacus held in the Roman psyche. Slaves in Rome were expected to accept their fate, but Spartacus represented resistance and rebellion against the slave society of Rome. Spartacus was the leader of the largest and most disruptive slave uprising in Roman history.

Spartacus' revolt began in 73 B.C. Spartacus was a part of a band of gladiators that escaped from their training school at Capua. Most of the slaves who were trained here were Gauls and Thracians. Spartacus was himself a Thracian. The slaves overtook the guards and escaped from the training school. They then armed themselves with weapons that they managed to seize from travelers on the nearby roads. They encamped themselves on Mount Vesuvius, raiding nearby settlements for supplies.

These rebel slaves were able to attract a large following of both fugitive slaves and even some free men. Oenomaus and Crixus, two fellow gladiators that escaped with Spartacus, served as his subordinate commanders. One of the things that helped attract followers to Spartacus was that he divided the profits from his raids equally. This sent a message of equality among Spartacus' men, which was a stark contrast to the elitism and rampant inequality of Rome.

The Romans sent a commander named Claudius Glaber to capture the rebels. Glaber blocked "the one narrow and difficult access road that led up the mountain." The other parts of the mountain were "formed of smooth and steep precipices," which would make escape for the slaves difficult. Glaber believed that he trapped the rebels, but the slaves managed to escape by creating ladders from the vines that they cut out. Plutarch explains:

> All the men, except one of them, descended safely by these devices. This one man stayed behind with the weapons. When the others had reached the bottom, he dropped the arms down. Only when all of them had been thrown down did he save himself last of all. The Romans were wholly unaware of these developments. Consequently, the slaves were able to surround them and to shock the Romans with a surprise attack.

The Romans fled and the slaves seized their camp. The slaves had managed to repel the first attempt by Rome to crush the rebellion. The Romans severely underestimated the rebelling slaves and for this reason they were not prepared to fight a real war. The result was that Spartacus defeated those forces. After this battle many more joined Spartacus' rebellion and his army numbered thousands of soldiers. Throughout the conflict some deserted from the Roman army, but Spartacus refused to accept defectors from the Roman army into his own army.

As recruits grew, Spartacus was able to build up an army. Florus explains:

> With the daily arrival of new recruits, they were finally able to form themselves into a regular army. They made rough shields for themselves out of vine branches covered with animal hides, and swords and spears by melting down and recasting their [leg] irons from the slave barracks.

Aside from building up an army to fight the Romans, Spartacus also engaged in customary Roman practices, including hosting gladiatorial contests between captured Roman soldiers. Returning again to Florus, he explains:

> He celebrated the deaths of his generals who had died in battle with funerary rituals usually reserved for regular army commanders. He ordered prisoners of war that his armies had captured to fight one another around the funeral pyres, hoping to demonstrate, I suppose, that he could expiate all his past shame by transforming himself into an exhibitor of gladiatorial contests.

The Romans then sent out Publius Varinius to combat Spartacus. Spartacus managed to outsmart Varinius by propping up corpses on stakes at the gates of the camp, so that the Romans believed night guards were stationed there. The rebels caught the Romans by surprise and in the ensuing conflict Spartacus managed to capture Varinius' horse. This defeat was a particularly humiliating one for Rome, which did not take the uprising seriously enough to even send the proper forces needed to put down the rebellion. Appian records:

These men did not command the regular citizen army of legions, but rather whatever forces they could hastily conscript on the spot, since the Romans did not yet consider this a real war but rather the raids and the predations of bandits. When they attacked Spartacus, however, they were defeated.

Following this victory, divisions within the rebel camp began emerging. Crixus wanted to march directly against the Romans to force a confrontation with them, but Spartacus was against this. Moreover, Crixus and some of the other slaves possessed a lust for revenge that was too great for even Spartacus himself to control. Some of the rebels began attacking unarmed civilians against the wishes of Spartacus. They raped both young girls and married women. Sallust explains that nothing "was either too sacred or too wicked to be spared the rage of these barbarians and their servile characters. Spartacus himself was powerless to stop them [...]." Orosius explains:

> Wherever they went, the slaves indiscriminately mixed slaughter, arson, theft, and rape. At the funeral rites of a woman whom they had taken prisoner and who had committed suicide because of her anguish over the violation of her sexual honor, they staged gladiatorial games, using four hundred prisoners they had taken. Those who had once been the spectacle were now to be the spectators [...].

This disunity proved to be costly to the uprising. Crixus decided to leave the slave camps to continue his war against the Romans. Rome dispatched two armies, one of which defeated Crixus' army. In the conflict two-thirds of Crixus' army perished along with Crixus himself. In an offering to Crixus, Spartacus sacrificed 300 Roman prisoners.

The war was now approaching its third year and had already

dragged on longer than the Romans expected. Appian wrote:

> This was now the third year of a war that had become particularly fearful for the Romans, although at the beginning they had treated it as a laughing matter and a contemptible thing, since it involved only gladiators.

The Romans decided to turn to Marcus Licinius Crassus to put down the uprising. One of the tactics that Crassus employed was to ensure that his men had more fear of him than they had of the rebel slaves. In his first encounter with the rebels, many of Crassus' men fled the battlefield out of fear. In response to this, it was said that Crassus selected every tenth man from the consular legions and had him executed because of the defeats that they suffered at the hands of the rebels. In total, it is believed that as many as four thousand men were executed. These tactics seemed to have worked because Crassus managed to defeat Spartacus' forces in the next encounter. Some of Spartacus' men had separated from him and set up a camp by themselves, where Crassus encountered them and killed about two-thirds of them.

This was the beginning of the end of Spartacus' rebellion. Crassus then marched against Spartacus. He defeated Spartacus in their conflict. Following this victory, Crassus pursued Spartacus to the seacoast where Spartacus was preparing to sail to Sicily. Spartacus was now trapped. He made an attempt to flee towards Samnite territory, but during this attempt Crassus managed to kill about 6,000 of Spartacus' troops. Rather than confronting the Romans with the full number of his forces, Spartacus resorted to surprise small-scale attacks. To demonstrate to his supporters the fate that awaited them if they lost, Spartacus crucified a Roman prisoner. Crucifixion was the punishment meted out to rebellious slaves. This must have been especially humiliating for the Romans to have one of their own soldiers executed in such a manner.

Pompey, who had just arrived from putting down an uprising in Spain, was sent to crush the rebellion. The Romans were eager to crush this slave rebellion, which they had initially underestimated. Appian explained that the Romans now realized that dealing with Spartacus was "a very difficult and substantial undertaking." Two of the advantages that Spartacus enjoyed in the initial phases of the rebellion were that the Romans had underestimated the gladiators and that many of the most skilled Roman generals, such as Pompey, were away fighting other battles. At this stage in the rebellion, however, Spartacus did not enjoy either of these advantages.

The involvement of Pompey in this conflict was also unfortunate for Crassus, who wanted the glory of putting down the slave rebellion for himself. Crassus was eager to force a confrontation with Spartacus to crush the rebellion. Spartacus was himself in a desperate situation. He attempted to negotiate a truce with Crassus, but to no avail. Spartacus was now in a dire situation in which both the armies of Crassus and Pompey were coming after him. Spartacus had no other option but to fight. When his horse was brought to him, Spartacus drew his sword and killed it. He told his followers that he would not need his horse. If they won the battle they would take the many horses of the Romans. If they lost the battle, he would have no need for a horse. In this Spartacus demonstrated that he had no intentions of fleeing. His plan seemed to have been leaving the battlefield victorious or not leaving the battlefield at all.

During the conflict with Crassus, Spartacus was wounded by a spear to his thigh. Spartacus continued fighting until the very end, however. Appian explained that the "killing was on such a scale that it was not possible to count the dead." In the aftermath of this final conflict Spartacus' body was never recovered and a number of his men escaped into the mountains, where they were pursued by Crassus' men. Many of the remaining rebels fought to the death. About six thousand were captured as prisoners. These prisoners were crucified "along the whole length of the highway that ran from Capua to Rome."

Crassus was the one who put down the rebellion, but about 5,000 rebels managed to escape his wrath. They were hunted down and killed by Pompey. Pompey then wrote to the senate explaining that he was the one who "extinguished the war to its very roots."

Although they were political rivals, Crassus and Pompey came to make up a political alliance known as the First Triumvirate, along with Julius Caesar.

The revolt of Spartacus would not be the last uprising on the part of gladiators. Tacitus recounted an uprising that occurred in 61 under the reign of Emperor Nero. Tacitus' record is also a testament to the manner in which Spartacus remained within the Roman psyche:

> At this same time, when gladiators in the town of Praeneste attempted a breakout, they were crushed by the unit of soldiers who manned the guard over them—but not before Spartacus and other evils of the past were bandied about in gossip by the people, eager and anxious as ever for revolutionary disturbances.

Conclusion

Prior to the development of the slave societies in the New World, similar slave societies existed in Greece and Rome. As was stated, the slave societies in Greece and Rome were not racial caste systems, but similarities did exist in a number of ways. For instance, in Athens citizenship was denied to even former slaves, much like freed blacks were denied full rights of citizenship in the United States. Slaves not only had no rights to citizenship, but were treated very brutally, which resulted in rebellion in a number of cases and even the creation of maroon societies formed by escaped slaves. The slave masters in the United States were not unaware of such similarities, which led to some examples of hypocrisy. The playwright Robert Montgomery Bird wrote a play dedicated to Spartacus in 1831, the same year that Nat Turner led a slave uprising against slave masters in Virginia. Bird, who praised the violent slave uprising of Spartacus, denounced the violence of African slaves, whom he saw as rebelling against the position that God had assigned for them:

> At this present moment there are 6[00] or 800 armed negroes marching through Southampton County, Virginia,

murdering, ravishing and burning those whom the Grace of God has made their masters—70 killed, principally women and children. If they had but a Spartacus among them—to organize the half million of Virginia, the hundreds of thousands of the states, and lead them on the Crusade of Massacre, what a blessed example might they not give to the excellence of slavery!

Moreover, we must keep in mind that America was a nation that was founded on the principle that "all men are created equal, that they are endowed by their Creator with certain unalienable Rights, that among these are Life, Liberty and the pursuit of Happiness." It should be no surprise that such principles did not extend to slaves, women, and people who did not own land. Slaves, women, and peasants were the same group of people that were unable to participate in Athenian democracy. Many of the Founding Fathers in America were influenced by Greece. John Adams, who served as America's second president, for instance, proclaimed that "the republics of Greece and Rome were the seats of liberty." Greece and Rome were perhaps seats of liberty for those who had the wealth and social standing to enjoy such liberty, but it certainly was not a land of liberty for the slaves. Likewise, America's ideals of democracy and liberty did not extend to slaves.

Pointing out such similarities is not to suggest that there is a direct link between the two systems. By the time that Europeans began enslaving African people the Roman Empire had long since collapsed. In the wake of the collapse of Rome, much of Europe transitioned into a system of feudalism. So this is not to suggest that there is any type of carryover from the period of Greek and Roman slavery in Europe, but rather to demonstrate that such slave societies did exist in Europe before they were established in the New World.

References:

Brent D. Shaw (editor), *Spartacus and the Slave Wars: A Brief History with Documents*, (University of Pennsylvania, 2001).

Deborah Kamen, "Sale for the Purpose of Freedom: Slave-Prostitutes and Manumission in Ancient Greece," *The Classic Journal*, 109.3, pp. 281-307, 2014.

Demetrios J. Constantelos, "American Philhellenism: Thomas Jefferson and the Influence of Greek Ideals and Culture in Writing the American Constitution," *Greek-American Review*, February 2002.

Lansiné Kaba, "The Atlantic Slave Trade Was Not a 'Black-on-Black Holocaust'", *African Studies Review*, Vol. 44, No. 1 (Apr., 2001), pp. 1-20

Peter Hunt, "Arming Slaves and Helots in Classical Greece," in *Arming Slaves in World History* (eds. Philip Morgan and Chris Brown), Yale University Press.

Robert K. Fleck and F. Andrew Hanssen, "Rulers Ruled by Women: An Economic Analysis of the Rise and Fall of Women's Rights in Ancient Sparta," September 2007.

Dr. Thomas Rüfner, "An Introduction to Roman Slave Law"

Walter Rodney, *A History of the Upper Guinea Coast, 1545 to 1800*, (Oxford University Press, 1970).

Walter Scheidel, "Slavery in the Roman Economy," September 2010.

www.ingramcontent.com/pod-product-compliance
Lightning Source LLC
Chambersburg PA
CBHW071348280526
45787CB00001B/259